HANDY REFERENCE

Toolbar Buttons in Excel

A summary of some of the toolbar buttons is given here for reference.

Click to create a new blank workbook.

New Button

Click to automatically total cells.

AutoSum Button

Click to open an existing workbook.

Open Button

Click to find and assemble the required function when building a formula.

Function Wizard Button

Click to preview the currently displayed workbook before printing it.

Print Preview Button

Double-click to display On-Line Help or the Answer Wizard.

Help Button

Shortcut Keys in Excel

These are some of the main keyboard shortcuts that will save you time when using Excel.

Action	Key	Action	Key
Undo last action	**Ctrl+Z**	Fill down	**Ctrl+D**
Repeat last action	**F4**	Fill to the right	**Ctrl+R**
Move to next sheet	**Ctrl+Page Down**	Calculate open workbooks	**F9**
Move to start of sheet	**Ctrl+Home**	Check spelling	**F7**
Select entire column	**Ctrl+Spacebar**	Edit cell note	**Shift+F2**
Select entire row	**Shift+Spacebar**	Switch between displaying formulas and results	**Ctrl+`**
Select entire sheet	**Ctrl+A**		
Move cell range	**Drag**	Convert selected reference from relative to absolute to mixed.	**F4**

ABOUT THE SERIES

In easy steps series is developed for time-sensitive people who want results fast. It is designed for quick, easy and effortless learning.

By using the best authors in the field, and with our experience in writing computer training materials, this series is ideal for today's computer users. It explains the essentials simply, concisely and clearly - without the unnecessary verbal blurb. We strive to ensure that each book is technically superior, effective for easy learning and offers the best value.

Learn the essentials **in easy steps** - accept no substitutes!

Titles in the series include:

Title	Author	ISBN
Windows 95	Harshad Kotecha	1-874029-28-8
Microsoft Office	Stephen Copestake	1-874029-37-7
Internet UK	Andy Holyer	1-874029-31-8
CompuServe UK	John Clare	1-874029-33-4
CorelDRAW	Stephen Copestake	1-874029-32-6
PageMaker	Scott Basham	1-874029-35-0
Quicken UK	John Sumner	1-874029-30-X
Microsoft Works	Stephen Copestake	1-874029-41-5
Word	Scott Basham	1-874029-39-3
Excel	Pamela Roach	1-874029-40-7
Sage	Ralf Kirchmayr	1-874029-43-1
SmartSuite	Stephen Copestake	1-874029-42-3

To order or for details on forthcoming titles ask your bookseller or contact Computer Step on 01926 817999.

EXCEL
in easy steps

Pamela Roach

COMPUTER
STEP

In easy steps is an imprint of Computer Step
5c Southfield Road, Southam
Warwickshire CV33 OJH England
☎01926 817999

First published 1996
Copyright © 1996 by Computer Step

Notice of Liability
Every effort has been made to ensure that this book contains accurate
and current information. However, Computer Step and the author
shall not be liable for any loss or damage suffered by readers as a
result of any information contained herein.

Trademarks
Microsoft$_{®}$ and Windows$_{®}$ are registered trademarks of Microsoft
Corporation. All other trademarks are acknowledged as belonging to
their respective companies.

For all sales and volume discounts please contact Computer Step on
Tel: 01926 817999.

For translation rights and export orders write to the address above or
Fax: (+44) 1926 817005.

Printed and bound in England

ISBN 1-874029-40-7

Contents

CHAPTER ONE

Getting Started

This chapter describes the elements of the Excel screen, how to move around and enter information. It also covers some of the features of Excel's comprehensive 'Help' system.

Covers

Introduction to the Screen

It is assumed that Excel has been installed. Click on the Start button, then Programs, and select Excel from the menu to start it.

On first starting Excel, the opening screen will appear as shown below.

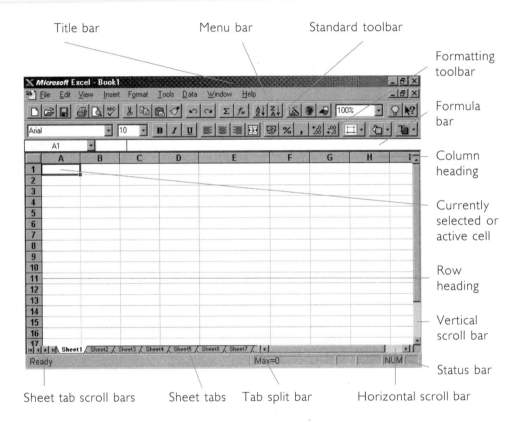

If the screen does not appear exactly like this, do not worry. It has probably arisen because Excel has already been used and the previous user has adjusted its format. Any such discrepancies can be corrected by using the techniques shown in the following sections.

Elements of the Screen

Refer to the opening screen, shown on the opposite page:

The Spreadsheet

This is the large central rectangular area which is subdivided into a grid of **cells**, used to store the spreadsheet data.

The Title Bar

This contains the title of the program and the name of the file which contains the spreadsheets and any associated charts, etc. It also contains at the left-hand end the button for the pull-down control menu. Remember that the easiest way to exit from Excel is to double-click this button with the left-hand mouse button.

The Menu Bar

This contains the menu names for all the commands used to build, format and control the spreadsheet. Clicking any menu name with the left mouse button will display a pull-down menu from which various options may be selected.

The Standard Toolbar

This contains a selection of 'buttons' representing the most commonly used commands required for standard tasks. These provide a more convenient and quicker way of accessing these commands, compared to using the menu bar.

The Formatting Toolbar

This contains a selection of 'buttons' representing the most commonly used commands required for formatting the contents of the spreadsheet. These again are usually faster although less comprehensive than using the menu bar.

The Formula Bar
This displays the location and the contents of the currently selected cell.

The Column Heading
This gives the horizontal location of each cell, the columns being labelled A, B, C, etc.

The Row Heading
This gives the vertical location of each cell, the rows being numbered 1, 2, 3, etc.

The Vertical Scroll Bar
This enables you to move the window vertically up and down the spreadsheet, under the control of the mouse.

The Horizontal Scroll Bar
This enables you to move the window horizontally to the left or right across the spreadsheet.

The Sheet Tab Scroll Bars
These enable you to control which sheet tabs are displayed.

The Sheet Tabs
These enable you to select which spreadsheet should be displayed.

The Tab Split Bar
This allows you to adjust the horizontal subdivision of space between the sheet tabs and the horizontal scroll bar.

Control of Window Options

The elements which appear in the window are controlled by two commands:

The **Options...** command from the **Tools** menu and

The **Toolbars...** command from the **View** menu.

The Options Command

1 Click Options from the Tools menu.

2 Click the View tab.

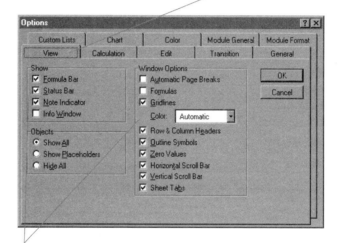

3 By clicking with the mouse, make sure that the following are checked, i.e. the respective check boxes contain ticks:

Show	Window Options
Formula Bar	Gridlines
Status Bar	Row and Column Headers
Note Indicator	Outline Symbols
	Zero Values
	Horizontal Scroll Bar
	Vertical Scroll Bar
	Sheet Tabs

The Toolbars Command

1 Click Toolbars from the View menu.

2 Make sure the 'Standard' and 'Formatting' options are ticked.

HANDY TIP

To strip the screen so it contains only the Title bar, Menu bar and Row and Column headings, select Full Screen from the View menu.

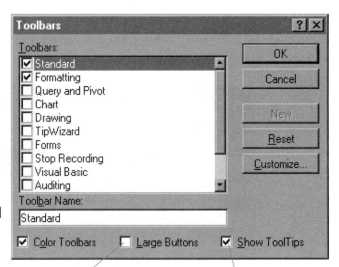

3 The Large Buttons option should be unticked, otherwise the screen may not display the full complement of buttons on toolbars.

4 Show ToolTips should be ticked to display descriptions of the buttons on the toolbars when resting the mouse pointer on a button.

5 Click OK and the screen should appear as shown at the beginning of this chapter. On exiting Excel, these settings will be retained for future use.

The Window on a Worksheet

What is a Workbook?

A workbook is a file which holds together a collection of worksheets (spreadsheets) and possibly chart sheets. It will be seen in later chapters that it is usual to have several spreadsheets linked together and often convenient to summarise the data on these spreadsheets in the form of charts or graphs.

What is a Worksheet (Spreadsheet)?

A worksheet or spreadsheet is an array of cells used to store data. This often involves simple arithmetic calculations linking the cells together in tables, usually for some kind of analysis.

The Window on a Worksheet

The opening Excel window displays initially:

     typically 9 columns labelled A to I

     typically 18 rows   labelled 1 to 18

– the exact number of rows and columns depending on the monitor screen size, driver and resolution.

It must be appreciated that this is only the extreme top left-hand corner of the full worksheet which extends to:

     256 columns   labelled A to Z, AA to IV

     16384 rows   labelled 1 to 16384

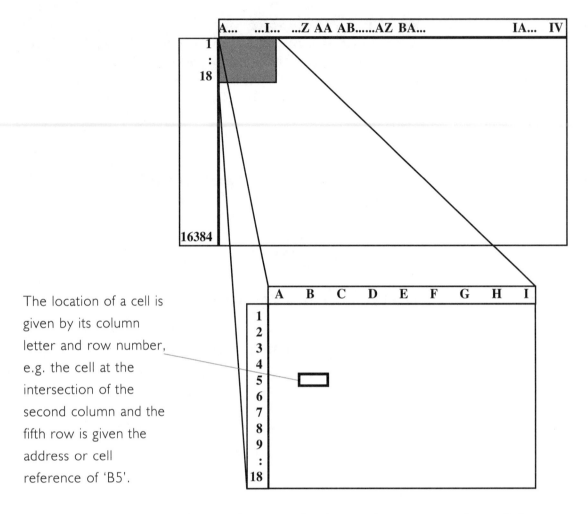

The location of a cell is given by its column letter and row number, e.g. the cell at the intersection of the second column and the fifth row is given the address or cell reference of 'B5'.

The Excel screen displays only a tiny window of the available worksheet.

Note that after labelling the first 26 columns A to Z, it is necessary to resort to double letters:

> AA to AZ

> BA to BZ etc...

resulting in cell references such as 'AB25'.

Keying in Data

Data can be entered into any cell in a worksheet in the following way:

1. In the worksheet, the mouse pointer is shaped like a cross. Position it over the destination cell and click the left mouse button to make the cell active. A border will appear around the cell and the cell reference will appear on the formula bar.

2. Key in the information required. The characters will appear simultaneously in the cell and on the formula bar.

3. Press the Enter key. The cursor will move to the next cell down.

Selecting Cells

Cells can be selected with the keyboard or the mouse. The following techniques illustrate selecting with the mouse:

Single cell	Point to cell and click left mouse button.
Multiple adjacent cells	Point to one extreme corner, hold down the left mouse button, and drag to the extreme opposite cell.
Multiple separated cells	Hold down the Control key while making the selections above.
Row(s)	Click a single row heading or many row headings.
Column(s)	Click a single column heading or many column headings.
Entire worksheet	Click the intersection of the row and column headings.

Moving Around

It is possible to move around a worksheet using the keyboard and the mouse.

Moving Using the Keyboard

The following keys can be used to position the cursor on the worksheet:

Key(s)	Alone	In combination with...
		Control
Up Arrow	Up one row	Up...
Down Arrow	Down one row	Down... to next filled region or to furthest row or column
Left Arrow	Left one column	Left...
Right Arrow	Right one column	Right...
		Control
Home	To beginning of row	To top left - cell A1
End	[Sets End mode]	Bottom right-hand corner of filled spreadsheet
End, Enter	Last cell in row [End followed by Enter]	
		Alt
Page Up	Up one screen (typically 18 rows)	Left one screen (typically 9 columns)
Page Down	Down one screen (typically 18 rows)	Right one screen (typically 9 columns)

...contd

Moving Using The Mouse

It is easy to scroll the window around the worksheet using the mouse on the scroll bars.

HANDY TIP **To move large distances with the mouse, hold down the Shift key while clicking the scroll bar.**

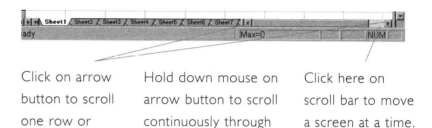

Click on arrow button to scroll one row or column at a time.

Hold down mouse on arrow button to scroll continuously through rows or columns.

Click here on scroll bar to move a screen at a time.

Moving Using Edit Go To

HANDY TIP **The Go To dialogue box is more appropriate for off-screen locations.**

An alternative technique of moving to a required cell is by means of the Go To command.

| Click Go To from the Edit menu.

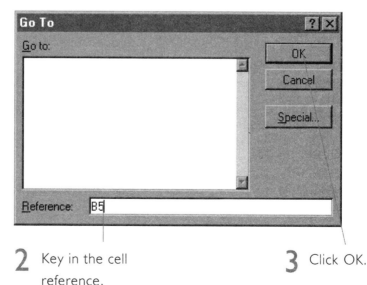

HANDY TIP **You can also enter the required cell reference on the formula bar and press Enter.**

2 Key in the cell reference.

3 Click OK.

Moving Between Worksheets

Using the Mouse

It is easy to switch between worksheets in the current workbook by using either the mouse or the keyboard.

1 Using the mouse, simply click on the required worksheet tab at the bottom of the display.

2 To display undisclosed worksheet tabs, use the tab scroll bars as shown below.

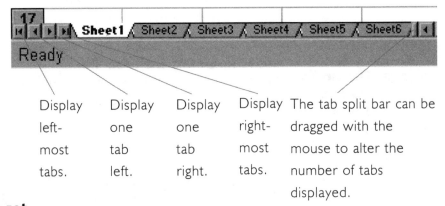

Display left-most tabs. | Display one tab left. | Display one tab right. | Display right-most tabs. | The tab split bar can be dragged with the mouse to alter the number of tabs displayed.

HANDY TIP

Do not get the keyboard commands confused with Alt plus Page Up or Page Down for moving the active cell horizontally by one screen.

Using the Keyboard

The keyboard code for changing the worksheet is to hold down the Control key and press Page Up or Page Down for left and right respectively.

Screen Tips

If there is an item on the screen on which you require some help, Screen Tips can be used to provide a brief explanation. They are available for commands, toolbar buttons, screen areas and dialogue boxes.

Screen Tips in a Dialogue Box

Click here.

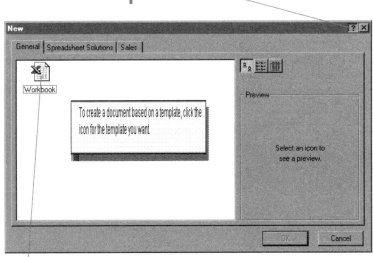

Tool Tips identify toolbar buttons when you point to them; you don't need to click the Help button first.

2 When the question mark appears on the cursor, click the item you want information on.

3 Click anywhere to close the information box.

Screen Tips using Help Button

Screen Tips can be activated by clicking the Help button.

When the question mark appears on the cursor, click the item you want information on.

The Tip Wizard

The Tip Wizard is represented by the electric light bulb icon on the right-hand side of the toolbar.

The Tip Wizard displays tips which can simplify and speed up the way you work. When there is a tip to be displayed, the light bulb icon will appear in yellow.

For example, if you were scrolling through a worksheet and you click the Tip Wizard button, you may see the following:

Click the Tip Wizard button.

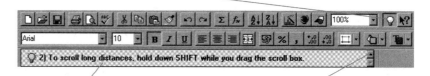

2 The tip will be displayed here.

3 Use the arrows to see other tips from the work session.

The Answer Wizard

The Answer Wizard allows you to type in a question in your own words and displays on-line help to assist with your task. The Help may be a step-by-step procedure, a Screen Tip, a visual example or reference information.

To activate the Answer Wizard, either select Answer Wizard from the Help Menu or double-click the Help button. Then click the Answer Wizard tab.

REMEMBER **The Function key F1 can be pressed at any time to assist you with your current task.**

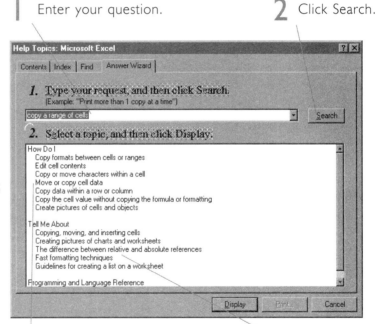

1 Enter your question.

2 Click Search.

3 Select a topic under How Do I if you want help completing the task, following the steps given by the Answer Wizard.

4 To understand the task better, select a task under Tell Me About.

The On-line Index

The on-line index can be used to provide the help you require.

1 Double-click the Help button and select the Index tab.

2 Type an entry.

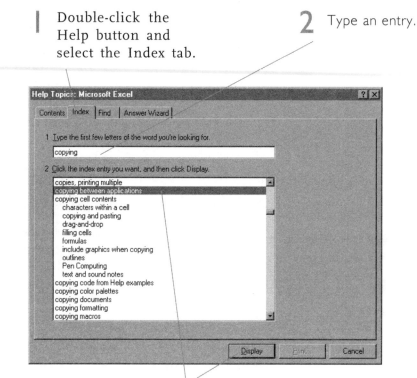

3 Select an entry and click Display.

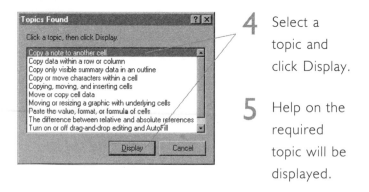

4 Select a topic and click Display.

5 Help on the required topic will be displayed.

CHAPTER TWO

Creating a Simple Spreadsheet

Covers

Keying in Data

Excel determines the type of data entered into a cell by the sequence of characters keyed. The types are:

To force a sequence of digits to be input as text, precede the digits by a single quote, e.g. as for a reference number '001234.

- Numbers (digits, decimal point, #, %, +, −)

- Text (any other string of characters)

- Formulas (First character entered is '=')

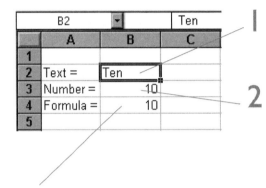

1 B2 contains text which is aligned to the left of the cell.

2 B3 contains the number 10 which is aligned to the right of the cell.

3 B4 contains the formula =6+4, which has been evaluated, and the resulting value, 10, is aligned to the right.

Displaying Formulas instead of Results

The normal default for spreadsheets is to display the results of evaluating formulas. To view the formulas stored:

A much quicker way of switching between the display of formulas and results is to hold down the Control key and press the open quote key (`) at the top left of the keyboard.

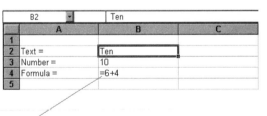

1 Click Options from the Tools menu.

2 On the View tab, check the Formulas box in Windows options.

3 Click OK and the formulas will be displayed.

Editing Data

Overtyping Cell Contents

The easiest way to edit data in a cell is to simply type a new entry over an existing one.

1   Select the cell to be changed.

2   Key in the new value or formula.

3   The new value is displayed as you enter it.

 In case you clear cells inadvertently, you can rectify your mistake by using the Undo command from the Edit menu or the standard toolbar.

Clearing Cell Contents

The easiest way to remove the contents of a cell and leave it blank is to select the cell and press the keyboard Delete key.

Editing Whilst Typing

If you notice that you have made a mistake and have not yet entered the information into the cell, you can edit using the following keys:

Backspace   to delete incorrect characters already typed in

Esc   to cancel data entry

Editing on the Formula Bar

If you have only mistyped part of a cell entry and only minor changes are needed, then editing can be done on the formula bar. The procedure is quite simple:

I Select the cell for editing, e.g. A2

2 The formula bar will display the current cell reference and its contents.

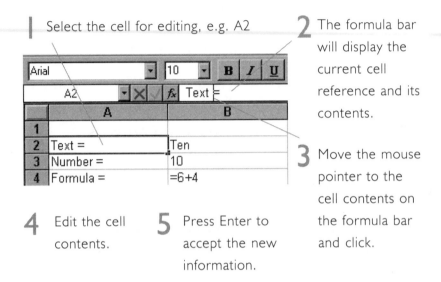

3 Move the mouse pointer to the cell contents on the formula bar and click.

4 Edit the cell contents.

5 Press Enter to accept the new information.

Editing at the Cell

An alternative technique to editing on the formula bar is to edit the contents of a cell at the cell itself.

I Point to the cell to be edited and double-click the left mouse button. The contents of the cell will be displayed.

2 Edit the contents of the cell.

3 Press Enter and the new value will be displayed.

HANDY TIP

To enable editing directly in the cell, click Options from the Tools menu, select the Edit tab and click the Edit Directly in Cell box.

AutoCorrect

The AutoCorrect feature of Excel allows the correction of common mistakes as you type. For example, consider the word *normally* – this is often misspelt as *normaly.*

 From the Tools menu, select AutoCorrect.

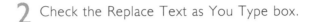 Check the Replace Text as You Type box.

3 Enter the commonly misspelt word.

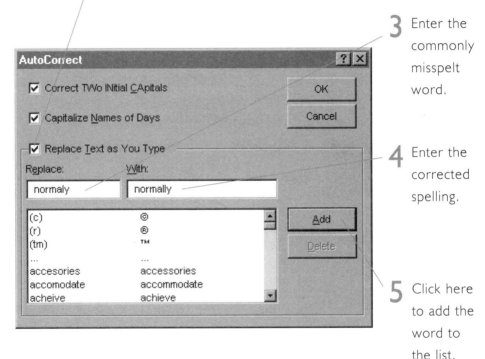

4 Enter the corrected spelling.

5 Click here to add the word to the list.

HANDY TIP

AutoCorrect can also be used to set up abbreviations to save typing. For example Q1 could always be replaced with Quarter1.

6 Press OK.

7 If *normaly* is typed into a cell, it will be automatically replaced by *normally.*

AutoComplete

The AutoComplete feature of Excel allows you to type just a few letters in a cell and the entry is completed based on entries already made in the column.

1 Enter start of column.

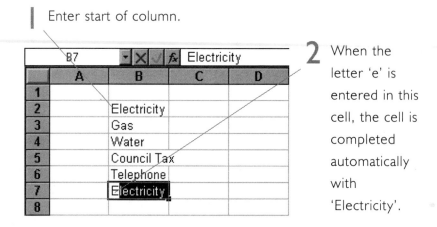

2 When the letter 'e' is entered in this cell, the cell is completed automatically with 'Electricity'.

Alternatively, the entry can be selected from a list.

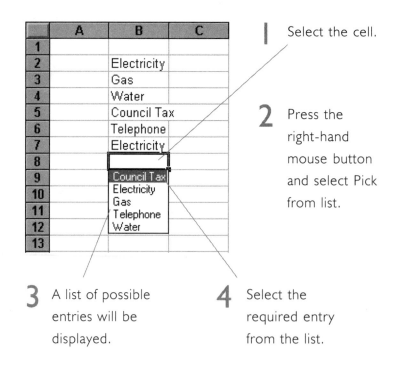

1 Select the cell.

2 Press the right-hand mouse button and select Pick from list.

3 A list of possible entries will be displayed.

4 Select the required entry from the list.

Planning a Spreadsheet Layout

When starting a new spreadsheet, it is necessary to decide on a strategy for the layout. In the example below, the text which forms the labels occupies far more space than the numbers and formulas. You need to decide how to store this information:

1   Widen Column – In some cases it is better to allocate one column to store all such text and adjust its width accordingly. The problem with this is that subsequent lines in this column cannot be subdivided into further columns.

	A	B	C	D
1		Units Used =	425	
2		Price per Unit =	0.073	
3		VAT Rate =	0.08	
4		Amount Due Excluding VAT =		

HANDY TIP

It is more flexible to allow wide labels to straddle several cells.

2   Allow Text to Straddle Columns – In other cases it is easier to allow such text to straddle several columns as shown below. However you must leave sufficient empty adjacent cells to fully display the text.

	A	B	C	D	E	F
1		Units Used =			425	
2		Price per Unit =			0.073	
3		VAT Rate =			0.08	
4		Amount Due Excluding VAT =				

Formatting Numbers

For speed, use the currency icon on the Formatting toolbar.

1 The three values: Units Used, Price per Unit and VAT Rate are entered as shown on the previous page. Price per Unit is a monetary figure and should be displayed in pounds and pence.

2 To format as currency, select the cell E2 and from the Format menu, click the Cells option.

3 Select the Number tab and select Category Currency.

4 Change Decimal Places to 3.

5 Click OK.

Alternatively, the price per unit could have been entered as £0.073.

The number of decimal places can be altered by using these icons on the Formatting toolbar:

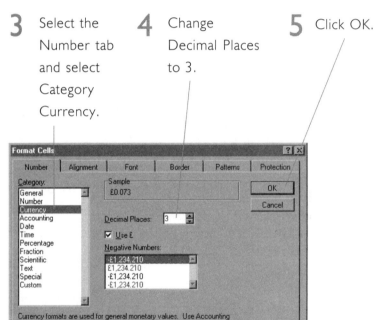

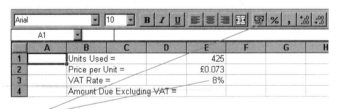

6 Select the VAT Rate and Format as Percentage by clicking the % icon on the Formatting toolbar.

Inputting Formulas

The Amount Due Excluding VAT is a formula which calculates the result of Units Used multiplied by the Price per Unit.

1 Select the cell which is to contain the formula, i.e. E4.

2 Press the equals key (=).

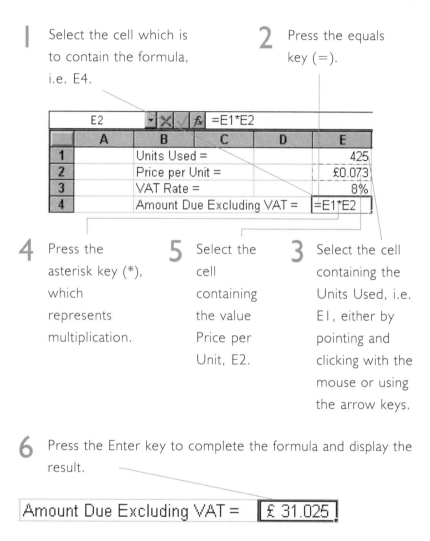

4 Press the asterisk key (*), which represents multiplication.

5 Select the cell containing the value Price per Unit, E2.

3 Select the cell containing the Units Used, i.e. E1, either by pointing and clicking with the mouse or using the arrow keys.

6 Press the Enter key to complete the formula and display the result.

Amount Due Excluding VAT = £ 31.025

Simple What-If Tests

The power of a spreadsheet is only really appreciated when you carry out 'What-If' tests. These involve adjusting the numbers in selected cells in order to observe the effect on formulas throughout the worksheet. Any such changes ripple through the worksheet.

B	C	D	E
Units Used =			425
Price per Unit =			£0.073
VAT Rate =			8%
Amount Due Excluding VAT =			£ 31.025

Increase the Units Used from 425 to 560 and this will affect the Amount Due which is calculated using Units Used.

Such changes should occur immediately. If not, click Options from the Tools menu, click the Calculation tab and uncheck Manual.

B	C	D	E
Units Used =			560
Price per Unit =			£0.073
VAT Rate =			8%
Amount Due Excluding VAT =			£ 40.880

2 Similar tests could be made by adjusting the Price per Unit.

B	C	D	E
Units Used =			1400
Price per Unit =			£0.073
VAT Rate =			8%
Amount Due Excluding VAT =			########

3 Increase the Units Used to 1400 and this will result in this error message (see the next section).

Adjusting Column Widths

The error message '#####' indicates that the cell width is insufficient to display the cell contents.

Adjusting Column Width Using Format Menu

Columns can be selected by holding down the Ctrl key while the headings are clicked.

1 Select the columns by clicking the respective headings.

2 From the Format menu, select Column.

3 From the Column sub-menu, select Width.

4 In the Column Width dialogue box, key in the width required.

5 Click OK.

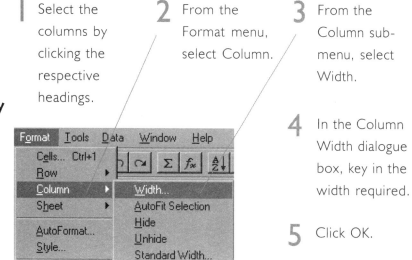

Adjusting Column Width Using the Mouse

Double-clicking the mouse whilst pointing to the right-hand margin of the column heading will adjust the column width to automatically accommodate the contents of the cell.

1 Point to the right-hand margin of the column heading. The pointer will change to a double-headed arrow.

Width:10.14		1400			
	A	B	C	D	E	F
1		Units Used =			1400	
2		Price per Unit =			£0.073	
3		VAT Rate =			8%	
4		Amount Due Excluding VAT =			########	
5						

2 Drag with the mouse to increase column width. The exact width will be displayed on the formula bar.

Inserting Rows and Columns

Don't worry about cell reference changes when inserting extra rows or columns – they will be adjusted automatically.

If, after you have set up your spreadsheet, you wish to add extra information in the middle of it, you may add extra columns or rows.

To add two rows after row 2, select rows 3 and 4 by pointing to the row headings and dragging.

	A	B	C	D	E	F
1		Units Used =			425	
2		Price per Unit =			£0.073	
3		VAT Rate =			8%	
4		Amount Due Excluding VAT =			£ 31.025	
5						

2 Click Rows from the Insert menu.

An alternative method of inserting extra rows/columns is to click the selected rows/ columns with the right mouse button and select Insert from the shortcut menu.

	A	B	C	D	E
1		Units Used =			425
2		Price per Unit =			£0.073
3					
4					
5		VAT Rate =			8%
6		Amount Due Excluding VAT =			£ 31.025
7					

3 The old rows 3 and 4 are displaced downwards by two rows to rows 5 and 6, leaving two blank rows.

The method for inserting extra columns is identical. The columns are highlighted by pointing at the column headings and dragging, then selecting Columns from the Insert menu.

Deleting Rows and Columns

Select the rows/columns by pointing to the row/column headings and dragging.

2 Either click the right mouse button and select Delete, or click Delete from the Edit menu.

If you delete rows or columns, be careful that you do not delete cells which are needed, e.g. those referred to in formulas or those containing data further down the column or row which you cannot see.

CHAPTER THREE

Copying and Moving Cells

If information is entered into the wrong cells accidentally, instead of deleting it and starting again, the cells can be moved somewhere else in the worksheet. Similarly, copying can be used to repeat data somewhere else in the worksheet. This chapter looks at the techniques of copying and moving cells both within a worksheet and between worksheets and of generating data automatically.

Covers

Copying and Moving Cells

1 Select the block of cells by dragging from corner to corner.

HANDY TIP

To copy the cells instead of moving them, hold down the Ctrl key whilst dragging the selected range to a new location.

B2	▾	Six=			
	A	B	C	D	E	F
1						
2		Six=	6			
3		Four=	4			
4		Product=	24			
5						
6						

2 Point to the border. The pointer will change from a cross to an arrow.

3 Press the left mouse button and drag to the new location. The outline of the selection will move whilst dragging.

HANDY TIP

An alternative method of copying or moving cells is to use the Cut, Copy and Paste commands. Select the block of cells to be copied or moved and press the right-hand mouse button to display the shortcut menu.

D2	▾	Six=			
	A	B	C	D	E	F
1						
2				Six=	6	
3				Four=	4	
4				Product=	24	
5						
6						

As well as moving the text, numbers and the formula, Excel also adjusts the formula so that it gives the correct cell references for its new location. In the original location, the formula in cell C4 was C2 * C3. In the new location, it has been changed to E2 * E3.

Copying Between Worksheets and Workbooks

A range of cells can easily be moved or copied between worksheets and workbooks.

Moving and Copying to another Worksheet

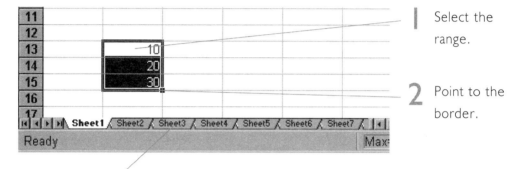

1 Select the range.

2 Point to the border.

3 To move, hold down the Alt key and drag to the other worksheet tab.

4 To copy, hold down the Alt key and the Ctrl key and drag to the other worksheet tab.

Moving and Copying to another Workbook

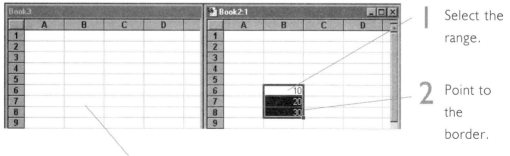

1 Select the range.

2 Point to the border.

3 To move, drag to a visible workbook window. To copy, hold down the Ctrl key whilst dragging.

Entering Data Automatically

It is possible to enter the same information in adjacent cells or enter an incremental series.

Copying the Same Data to Adjacent Cells

1 Select the cells containing the data

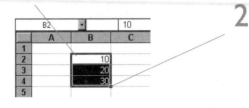

2 Point to the fill handle, whilst pressing down the Ctrl key. The pointer will change to +.

3 Drag the selection down to the cells which require filling. The data is copied to the rest of the cells.

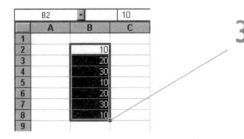

A series can be numerals, e.g. 10, 20, 30 etc. times or dates, e.g. January, February etc., or ordinals, e.g. first, second etc.

Generating a Series

1 Enter the beginning of the series and select the entries.

	A	B	C	D	E	F
1						
2		Mon	Tue			
3						

2 Drag the AutoFill handle.
DO NOT press the Ctrl key.

3 The rest of the days of the week are filled in automatically.

	A	B	C	D	E	F	G
1							
2		Mon	Tue	Wed	Thu	Fri	
3							

Using the Series Dialogue Box

The Series dialogue box gives a much greater degree of control than using the AutoFill handle. To use the Series dialogue box, carry out the following:

1 Click Fill from the Edit menu and then click Series.

or

Click the right-hand mouse button whilst dragging the AutoFill handle. A shortcut menu will be displayed from which the Series option can be selected.

2 Select type of series.

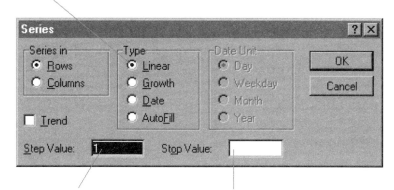

3 Enter Step Value.

4 If you are uncertain of the number of items in a series, key in the Stop Value to terminate the series.

5 Click OK.

Creating your own AutoFill Lists

If your application frequently uses lists of text, then it will pay you to make it into a custom list for use under AutoFill.

1 Select the list on the worksheet.

2 From the Tools menu, select Options and click the Custom Lists tab. Note that lists for months and days of the week are already shown.

HANDY TIP

You can create a new list by typing the entries into the List Entries box, pressing Enter after each. When complete click Add.

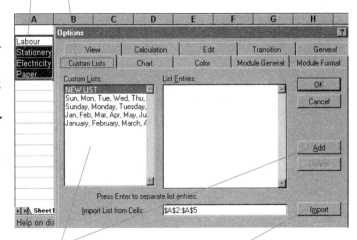

4 Click Add so that the new list appears under Custom Lists.

3 Click Import and the list will appear under List Entries.

5 Click OK to finish.

6 To use your list, simply apply AutoFill to any single word.

CHAPTER FOUR

Managing Workbook Files

Excel provides an extensive range of features for creating, finding, opening and saving workbook files.

Covers

Saving a New File

The File Save As command is used to save a new file to disk.

1 Click on Save As from the File menu, or on the standard toolbar click the Save button.

HANDY TIP

Use Save As to copy a file by giving it another name/ location.

2 Click here to display other drives.

These icons are explained on the next page.

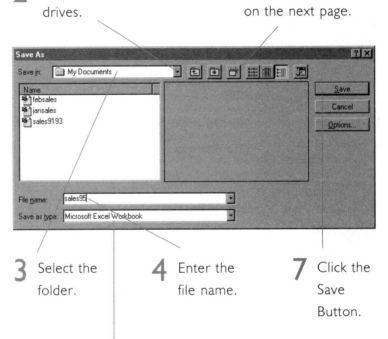

REMEMBER

It is possible to convert Excel files to other popular spreadsheet or database formats by selecting the required format in the Save as Type list.

3 Select the folder.

4 Enter the file name.

7 Click the Save Button.

5 Accept Microsoft Excel Workbook as type.

6 If you wish a backup file to be created automatically when the file is saved, click Options and check the Always Create Backup box.

...contd

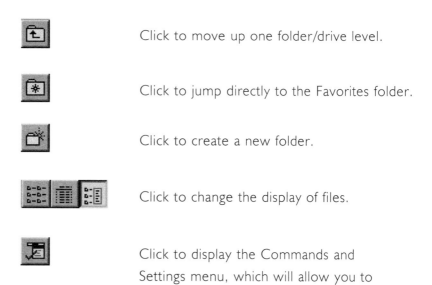

Click to move up one folder/drive level.

Click to jump directly to the Favorites folder.

Click to create a new folder.

Click to change the display of files.

Click to display the Commands and Settings menu, which will allow you to sort files, add properties to a selected file or map to a network drive.

Favorites Folder

The Favorites folder is used to store shortcuts to workbooks which are opened frequently without having to remember where the file is located.

My Documents Folder

The My Documents folder is located at the root level of the hard disk and is a good place to store files that are currently being worked on. It is the default folder which is displayed when the Save As dialogue box and the Open dialogue box (see later section) are first displayed.

File Properties

Entering file properties will allow a file to be located more easily. Excel automatically sets some file properties such as the author's name and the date the file was created, but others can be defined.

Click Properties from the File menu.

or

Click the File Properties icon on the Save As dialogue box.

To automatically prompt for properties when a file is first saved, check the Prompt for File Properties box under Options... General from the Tools menu.

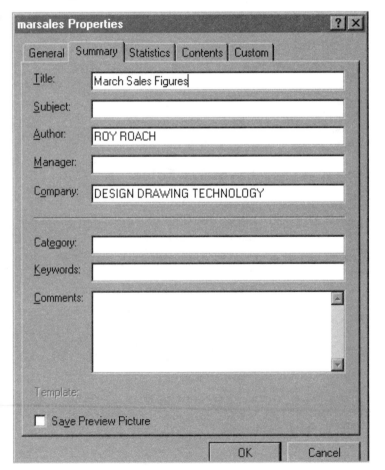

2   Type in properties which will group workbooks so they can be located easily at a later date.

Saving Existing Files

File Save Command

This command is used to save changes to the current workbook replacing the existing version.

If the file has not been saved before, then the Save As dialogue box will be displayed. Otherwise there will be a short delay, indicated by the pointer changing to the Timer icon, after which you may resume your work.

| Click Save from the File menu.

or

Click the Save button on the standard toolbar.

AutoSave

It is possible to set up Excel to remind you at regular intervals to save your work. To use the AutoSave command, carry out the following:

| Click the AutoSave option from the Tools menu.

2 Switch on AutoSave by checking the Automatic Save box.

AutoSave is an Add-In Command which may not be installed. To install it, select Add-Ins from the Tools menu and check AutoSave.

3 Enter interval between automatic saves.

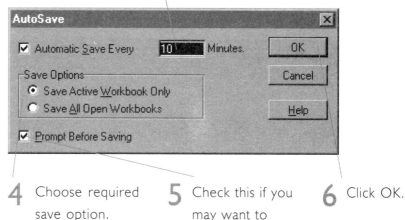

4 Choose required save option.

5 Check this if you may want to override saves.

6 Click OK.

Opening Files

To save yourself entering the folder location each time you open a file, enter the default folder location in Options... General from the Tools menu.

1 Click Open from the File menu.

or

Click the Open button on the standard toolbar.

2 Select a folder to look in.

3 Look in Favorites folder.

4 Click to display a thumbnail view of the selected workbook.

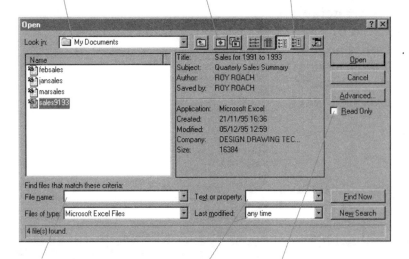

The File menu can be set up so that it lists the most recently used files by checking the Recently Used File List box in Options... General from the Tools menu.

5 Enter any part of the file name here.

6 Check the Read Only box to open the selected workbook so that it can be viewed without making changes to it.

7 Searches can be carried out by specifying criteria in these two boxes.

8 Click the Advanced button to enter precise search criteria to allow files to be located easily. The searches can be saved and used again at a future date.

Creating Workbooks

Creating new workbooks is made easy by the provision of templates. A template is a predesigned workbook which is ready to use. As well as using the templates provided, you can design your own and create sets of templates. Alternatively you can create a new blank worksheet.

1 Click New from the File menu.

2 For a blank worksheet, click the General tab and double-click the Workbook icon.

3 Click other tabs to browse available templates.

When you use a template to create a workbook by selecting New from the File menu, the original template remains unchanged.

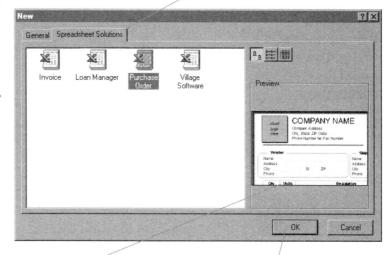

4 Select a template and a thumbnail view appears.

5 Click OK to create a workbook from the selected template.

Saving Workbooks as Templates

Workbooks can be saved as templates, by selecting Template format from the Save as type drop-down list box in the Save As dialogue box.

If the workbook is saved in the Templates folder, it will appear on the General tab on the New dialogue box. Additional tabs can be created by adding an extra folder to the Templates folder.

1 Select Templates folder to place template on General tab.

2 Click here to add a new folder to Templates folder.

Built-in templates can be customized by clicking the Customize button on the template.

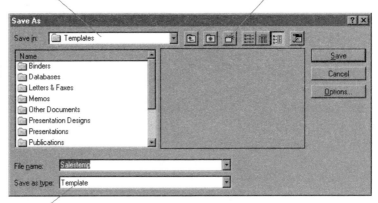

3 Select Template as Save as type.

4 Creating a new folder within templates creates an additional tab as long as it contains at least one template.

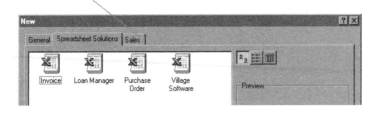

Closing Files and Exiting Excel

File Close

1 This closes the active workbook.

2 If any changes have been made since it was last saved, then the dialogue box below will appear.

3 Excel is left running, either with the remainder of the open workbooks or with no workbooks open.

File Exit

1 This closes all active workbooks.

2 If any changes have been made to any Workbook since it was last saved, then the dialogue box below will appear.

3 Excel is shut down.

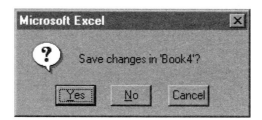

If Yes is selected, the workbook is saved. If it hasn't previously been saved, the Save As dialogue box will be displayed.

If No is selected, any changes to the workbook made since it was last saved will be lost.

File Save Workspace

Some applications require that several workbooks are open and that various worksheets are displayed simultaneously. The setting up of the workspace, i.e. the workbooks to be opened, the windows to be displayed and their various sizes and positions can be very time-consuming. To avoid repeating these operations, the workspace can be saved.

HANDY TIP

The default filename for a workspace file is Resume.XLW.

1 Click Save Workspace from the File menu.

2 Select a folder.

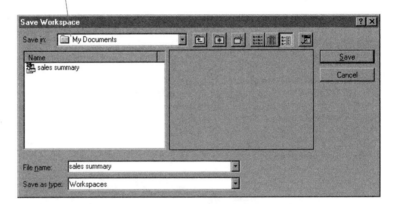

HANDY TIP

To open the workspace automatically when starting Excel, copy it to the Startup Directory (see the Tools Options General tab dialogue box).

3 Enter filename.

4 The file type is Workspaces, which have the .XLW extension.

5 Click Save.

6 Subsequently, the file Sales Summary can be opened, which will restore the workspace.

Managing Documents

From the File Open dialogue box, a shortcut menu can be displayed which allows documents to be copied, moved, deleted etc.

1 Select Open from the File menu.

2 Click a document name and press the right-hand mouse button once.

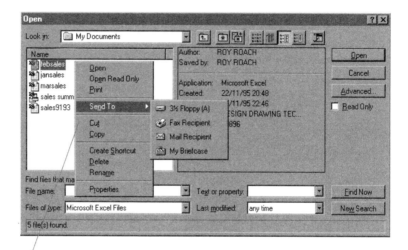

3 A shortcut menu will be displayed.

4 Select a command from the shortcut menu.
The commands are explained on the following page.

Open – Opens the file and allows changes to be made.

Open Read Only – Opens the file as read only.

Print – Allows selected file to be printed.

Send To – Allows selected file to be copied to floppy disk, or sent via Microsoft fax, Microsoft mail (if these features are installed on your computer) or copied to My Briefcase.

Cut – Allows selected file to be moved.

Copy – Allows file to be copied to another filename.

Create Shortcut – Allows a quick access to the file to be created.

Delete – Allows selected file to be deleted. A warning message will be issued asking for confirmation to move file to Recycle bin.

Rename – Allows selected file to be renamed. The cursor is moved to filename and edit mode is entered allowing you to change the name.

Properties – Displays file properties, e.g. size, when updated etc. and attributes, e.g. read, write etc.

CHAPTER FIVE

Cell Referencing

Excel has different methods of referencing cells. This chapter gives examples of these different methods.

Covers

Relative References

A relative reference such as E3 = C3*D3 tells Excel where to locate a cell, starting from the cell containing the formula. Consider the following example where:

Amount Due = Unit Price * Units Used

	A	B	C	D	E	F
1						
2		**Product**	**Unit Price**	**Units Used**	**Amount Due**	
3		Electricity	£ 0.07	425	£ 31.03	
4		Gas	£ 0.13	502	£ 62.75	
5		Water	£ 0.08	380	£ 30.40	
6						

E3 = C3*D3
This means, the value at E3 is equal to the contents of the cell which is located in the same row (row 3) but two columns to the left (column C) multiplied by the contents of the cell which also lies in the same row, but is in the column immediately to the left (column D).

The formula is copied to the adjacent rows by dragging the AutoFill Handle. The formula is automatically adjusted from C3*D3 to C4*D4 and C5*D5.

E
Amount Due
=+C3*D3
=+C4*D4
=+C5*D5

Absolute References

An absolute reference such as $B$1 tells Excel where to locate a cell given the exact location, i.e. row and column of that cell. Normally a copied formula will adjust the cells accordingly, but an absolute reference will remain unchanged, always pointing to the same cell. Consider the following example where VAT is calculated as:

Amount Due * VAT Rate

	A	B	C	D	E	F
1	VAT Rate=	8.0%				
2		Product	Unit Price	Units Used	Amount Due	VAT
3		Electricity	£0.07	425	£ 31.03	£ 2.48
4		Gas	£0.13	502	£ 62.75	£ 5.02
5		Water	£0.08	380	£ 30.40	£ 2.43
6						

HANDY TIP

To switch from a relative reference to an absolute reference, select the cell and press F4.

VAT is calculated as the contents of the cell immediately to the left multiplied by the contents of the cell in column B row 1. The cell containing VAT Rate remains the same for all calculations, therefore the absolute reference will always point to cell B1.

F
VAT
=+E3*$B$1
=+E4*$B$1
=+E5*$B$1

Mixed References

A mixed reference such as $B2 or B$2 tells Excel how to locate a cell based on a relative row reference and fixed column reference or a fixed row reference and relative column reference. $B2 references the cell where the column B is fixed and the row 2 is relative. B$2 references the cell where the column B is relative and the row 2 is fixed. Consider the following example of generating part of a multiplication table:

	A	B	C	D
1				
2		10	11	12
3	10	100	110	120
4	11	110	121	132
5	12	120	132	144
6				

| Select cell B3 and press =.

2 Point to cell A3 and click. Press F4 three times to change A3 to $A3. $A fixes the reference on column A.

3 Key in the multiplication symbol, an asterisk.

	A	B	C	D
1				
2		10	11	12
3	10	=+$A3*B$2	=+$A3*C$2	=+$A3*D$2
4	11	=+$A4*B$2	=+$A4*C$2	=+$A4*D$2
5	12	=+$A5*B$2	=+$A5*C$2	=+$A5*D$2
6				

4 Point to B2 and click. Press F4 twice to change B2 to B$2 and press Enter. $2 fixes the reference absolutely on row 2.

5 Drag the Fill handle on cell B3 across to cell D3 so that it copies the formulas. Drag the AutoFill handle on the selection B3:D3 down to row 5 so that it copies the formulas to adjacent rows.

R1C1 Referencing

There is an older alternative style of referencing cells, called the 'R1C1' method, by which both columns and rows are numbered. It has the advantage that the distinction between absolute and relative referencing is easier to understand. Its disadvantage is that it is not as brief as the A1 method, which is the default for Excel. The procedure for changing the reference style is:

1 Click Options from the Tools menu.

2 Click the General tab.

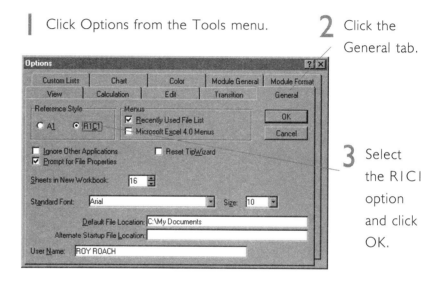

3 Select the R1C1 option and click OK.

A relative reference employs square brackets to indicate the offsets relative to the cell containing the formula. For example RC[-2] references the cell in the same row, but two columns to the left.

	5	6
1		
2	**Amount Due**	**VAT**
3	=+RC[-2]*RC[-1]	=+RC[-1]*R1C2
4	=+RC[-2]*RC[-1]	=+RC[-1]*R1C2
5	=+RC[-2]*RC[-1]	=+RC[-1]*R1C2
6		

In this style R1C2 means the absolute reference given by the intersection of row 1 and column 2.

Naming Cells

An alternative way of referencing cells is to give them a 'name' or identifier which describes the cells' contents. There are several advantages of using this method, the most obvious reason being, it is much easier to understand a formula expressed in words.

Defining Names Using the Name Box

The easiest way to define names for cells is to use the Name box on the formula bar. This is illustrated in the following example:

Names may be up to 255 characters. The first character must be a letter or underscore(_). Other characters may be any sequence of letters and digits. Separators must be either underscore or full stop. Names are not case sensitive.

1 Select the cell to be named, e.g. B1. Its reference will appear on the formula bar.

2 Click the Name box button on the formula bar to display the Name box, which at this stage will be empty.

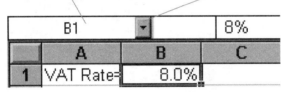

3 In place of the cell reference, 'B1', key in the name, say "VAT Rate", to represent this cell.

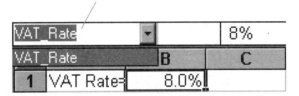

4 To confirm that it has been added to the list of names, click the button again to display the Name Box.

Pasting Names Using the Name Box

The easiest way to paste names into formulas is to use the Name box. Consider the following example:

1 Select the cell in which to store the formula, i.e. F3.

F3	▾	✕	✓	f_x	=E3*

VAT_Rate	B	C	D	E	F
1 VAT Rate=	8.0%				
2	**Product**	**Unit Price**	**Units Used**	**Amount Due**	**VAT**
3	Electricity	£0.07	425	£ 31.03	=E3*
4	Gas	£0.13	502	£ 62.75	
5	Water	£0.08	380	£ 30.40	

HANDY TIP

For long lists of names, type the first letter of the name to speed up its location.

2 Press '=' and point and click on cell E3 (Amount Due).

3 Press '*' for the multiplication symbol.

4 On the formula bar, click the name button to display the Name box.

5 Click the name VAT_Rate and it will appear in the formula.

6 Press Enter to complete the formula.

B1	▾	✕	✓	f_x	=E3*VAT_Rate

	A	B	C	D	E	F
1	VAT Rate=	8.0%				
2		**Product**	**Unit Price**	**Units Used**	**Amount Due**	**VAT**
3		Electricity	£0.07	425	£ 31.03	=E3*VAT_Rate
4		Gas	£0.13	502	£ 62.75	
5		Water	£0.08	380	£ 30.40	
6						

Naming Cell ranges

Ranges of cells, i.e. adjacent cells in rows, columns or blocks, can be named using the Name box in the same way as single cells.

Insert Name Sub-Menu

The Command menu bar offers more facilities for naming cells and applying cell names than the Name box on the formula bar.

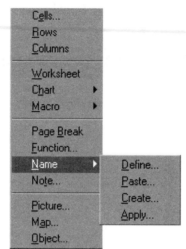

Define... enables new names to be defined and existing ones to be deleted.

Paste... enables names to be pasted into formulas.

Create... enables names to be created from column and/or row headings.

Apply... enables cell references in selected formulas to be replaced by the equivalent names.

 The Paste Name dialogue box can be used to paste names in formulas, although it is usually easier to use the Name box. However an additional use for it is to list on the worksheet all the names and cell references.

The Define Name Dialogue Box

1 Select the cell or range of cells to be named.

2 From the Insert menu and the Name sub-menu, click the Define... option.

3 Enter required name, or accept the name automatically proposed and click OK.

The Paste Name Dialogue Box

1 Select the cell or range of cells to be named.

2 From the Insert menu and the Name sub-menu, select the Define... option.

3 Click the Paste List button to paste a list of named cells.

...contd

The Create Names Dialogue Box

1 Select the range of cells to be named and the appropriate row and/or column headings.

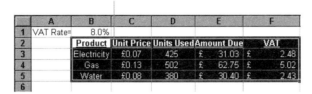

	A	B	C	D	E	F
1	VAT Rate=	8.0%				
2			Product	Unit Price	Units Used	Amount Due	VAT
3			Electricity	£0.07	425	£ 31.03	£ 2.48
4			Gas	£0.13	502	£ 62.75	£ 5.02
5			Water	£0.08	380	£ 30.40	£ 2.43
6							

2 From the Insert menu and the Name sub-menu, click the Create option.

3 Complete the dialogue box, by selecting the location of the table labels. E.g. in this example, select Top Row and click OK.

4 The created names will appear in the Name box on the formula bar.

The Apply Names Dialogue Box

1 From the Insert menu and the Name sub-menu, click the Create option.

Hold down the Ctrl key while clicking to select individual names.

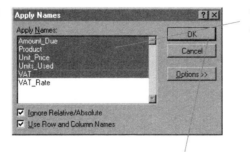

2 Select the cell names that are to be applied in formulas.

3 Click OK and the formulas will show names instead of cell references.

Using Cell Reference Operators

Cell reference operators are used to link cell references:

The Range operator (the colon ':') means the rectangular block of cells formed between the two cell references which it separates.

The Union operator (the comma ',') means the set of cells formed by the list of cell references which it separates. This list need not be consecutive.

The Intersection operator (the space ' ') means the cells defined at the intersection of the cell ranges that it separates. These ranges must overlap, otherwise an error message will appear.

	A	B	C	D	E	
1			Quarterly Sales			
2			1991 to 1993			
3						
4		Qtr1	Qtr2	Qtr3	Qtr4	
5	1991	£8,000	£10,000	£15,000	£12,000	
6	1992	£9,000	£11,000	£17,000	£13,000	
7	1993	£10,000	£12,000	£19,000	£14,000	
8						
9	Total Sales for 1992=				£50,000	=SUM(B6:E6)
10	Quarter 3 Sales for 1991 to 1993=				£51,000	=SUM(D5,D6,D7)
11	Quarter 3 Sales for 1992=				£17,000	=SUM(B6:E6 D5:D7)

E9 contains a reference to a range of cells.

E10 contains a reference to a list of cells.

E11 contains a reference to the intersection of two ranges.

CHAPTER SIX

Functions

Excel has a number of in-built functions which perform specialised calculations for wide-ranging applications e.g. statistical, mathematical, financial, etc. The most commonly used functions are available using the new AutoCalculate feature.

Covers

Overview

Functions are easy to recognise because they are always followed by open and close brackets. For example:

SUM(range)   Adds together a range of numbers.

AVERAGE(range)   Finds the average of a range of numbers.

MAX(range)   Finds the largest number in a range.

MIN(range)   Finds the smallest number in a range.

The Function Wizard

The Function Wizard can be used to help find and assemble the required function when building a formula. The Function Wizard can be activated in two possible ways:

| Click Function from the Insert menu.

  or

2 Click the Function Wizard button on the standard toolbar.

The Function Wizard dialogue boxes are presented in two stages, the first to guide you to choose the function name, the second to guide you to fill in the appropriate arguments or cell range. The use of these two dialogue boxes will be illustrated later on in this chapter.

The SUM Function

The SUM function can be used to automatically total adjacent cells. This function can be quickly accessed by clicking the **AutoSum** button on the standard toolbar.

Σ

1   Select the cell where the total is to appear.

2   Click the AutoSum button on the standard toolbar.

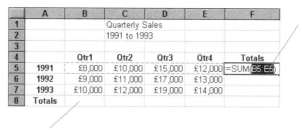

3   The SUM function is created, totalling values for 1991.

4   Totals for Qtr1 can be created by clicking here and clicking AutoSum.

Alternatively, all quarters and years could be totalled at once as follows:

1   Select the whole table including cells where totals are to be placed.

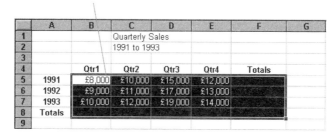

2   Click the AutoSum button.

The LOOKUP Function

The following example illustrates the use of a LOOKUP table and the Function Wizard.

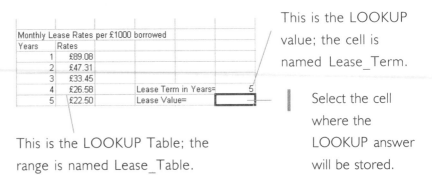

This is the LOOKUP value; the cell is named Lease_Term.

Select the cell where the LOOKUP answer will be stored.

This is the LOOKUP Table; the range is named Lease_Table.

2 Click the Function Wizard button on the standard toolbar.

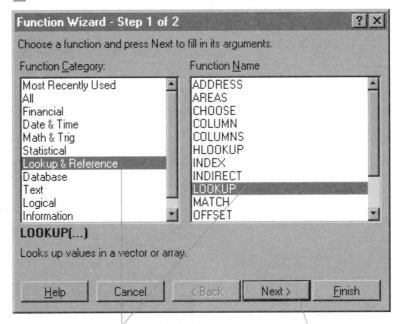

When you have used several functions, the Most Recently Used category will prove useful since it stores the names of the last ten functions used.

3 Click Lookup & Reference as Function Category and LOOKUP as Function Name.

4 Click Next to proceed to next dialogue box.

5 Complete the intermediate dialogue box for this function. Select lookup_value, array and click OK.

6 Click the Name box button on the formula bar and click Lease_Term.

To view the Name box and cells, you may have to move the Function Wizard dialogue box by dragging its title bar.

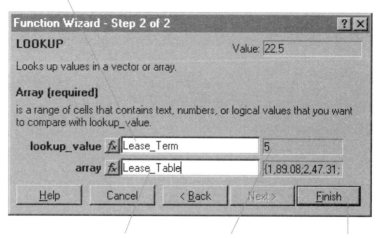

Instead of names, cell references can be used.

8 Click Lease_Table on the Name box. The values stored in the table appear in the dialogue box.

The value stored in the cell named Lease_Term appears here.

9 Click the Finish button to complete the function.

7 Press the Tab key to move to the next argument, the table to be searched.

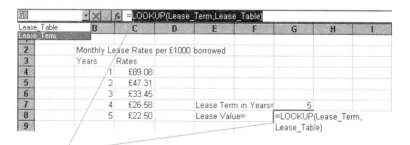

10 The function is displayed in the selected cell and on the function bar.

The IF Function

The IF() function is found in the Logical category of the Function Wizard. It can be described in simple terms as:

IF (condition, action if condition true, action if condition false)

The condition is a logical test which uses logical or comparison operators. These are:

=	equal to	<>	not equal to
>	greater than	>=	greater than or equal to
<	less than	<=	less than or equal to

A conditional formula will contain one or more comparison operators. E.g.,

C6 > 12   tests whether cell C6 is greater than 12.

B4 <= G8 tests whether cell B4 is less than or equal to cell G8.

Using the IF Function

Consider the following example where we wish to work out how much discount each customer is entitled to. The condition is:

If the amount they have spent is greater or equal to £1000, then the discount is 20%. If the amount they have spent is less than £1000 then the discount is 10%.

	A	B	C	D
1		Customer Discount Figures		
2				
3		Name	Amount Spent	Discount
4				
5		Brierley	£1,280	
6		Jones	£1,020	
7		Mitchell	£570	
8		Harrison	£1,150	
9		Wood	£870	

Select the cell required.

2 Click the Function Wizard button on the standard toolbar.

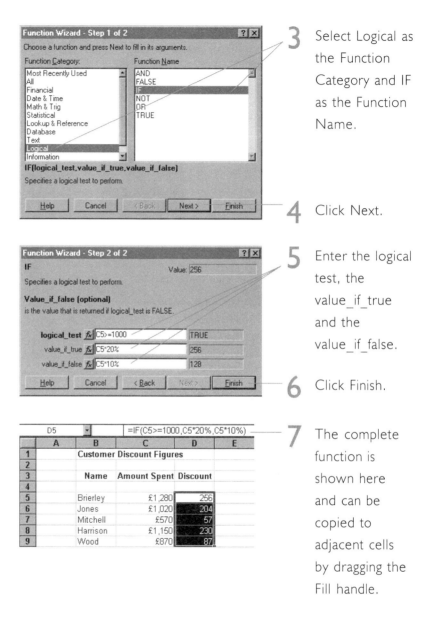

3 Select Logical as the Function Category and IF as the Function Name.

4 Click Next.

5 Enter the logical test, the value_if_true and the value_if_false.

6 Click Finish.

7 The complete function is shown here and can be copied to adjacent cells by dragging the Fill handle.

AutoCalculate

The AutoCalculate feature displays the answer to a function in a status bar at the bottom of the screen.

1 Select the range of cells.

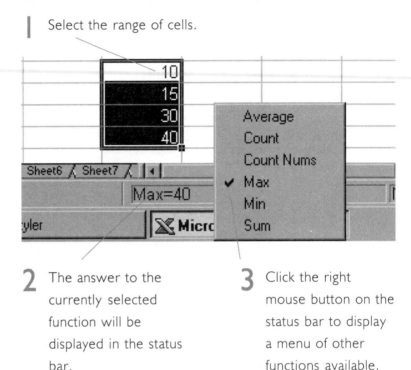

2 The answer to the currently selected function will be displayed in the status bar.

3 Click the right mouse button on the status bar to display a menu of other functions available.

CHAPTER SEVEN

Cell Errors and Auditing

If Excel fails to evaluate a formula in a cell, then it displays an error message. This chapter illustrates some of these errors so that when they occur you will have a better idea of what is causing them. Excel also provides a set of auditing tools to help trace errors.

Covers

Cell Errors

In the following examples, all the errors have been generated deliberately. On the left is the data, with the resulting error values. On the right are displayed the formulas:

(1) **#DIV/o!**   This error is caused by an attempt to divide 2.5 by zero. Theoretically this should generate infinity. In practice any such value is too big, even for a computer, and the calculation is suppressed.

(2) **#N/A**   This means that **N**o value is **A**vailable, since the first argument of the LOOKUP function is cell B8 which contains text, instead of D8 which contains a number.

(3) **#NAME?**   Excel fails to recognise the Name of the function 'IS', which has been incorrectly typed for 'IF'.

	A1	⬇		'(1)			D
	A	**B**	**C**	**D**		**D**	
1	(1)						
2		2.5	0	#DIV/0!		=B2/C2	
3							
4	(2)						
5	Amount:	£0	£500	£1,000		1000	
6	Discount:	0.0%	5.0%	10.0%		0.1	
7							
8		Price =		£750		750	
9		Discount Rate =		#N/A		=LOOKUP(B8, B5:D6)	
10							
11	(3)						
12		-0.25		#NAME?		=IS(B12=0, "Zero", "Non-zero")	
13							
14	(4)						
15		5	10	15		15	
16	2						
17	4						
18	6			#NULL!		=B15:D15 A16:A18	

(4) **#NULL!** This formula (on the previous page) uses the **intersection operator** (a space) to locate the cell at the intersection of ranges B15:D15 and A16:A18. Since they do not intersect, Excel displays the error message.

(5) **#NUM!** This error value indicates problems with numbers. The first example of this error (see below) attempts to generate the value 100^{1000}, i.e. 100 multiplied by itself 1000 times, which is too large for the computer to store and the calculation is suppressed.

In the second example the attempt to calculate the square root (SQRT function) of a negative value is suppressed.

(6) **#VALUE!** This error occurs when the data in a cell isn't appropriate for the operation, or the operation doesn't apply to the type of data. Here an attempt has been made to divide 'Text' by 50.

(7) **######** This error is not necessarily generated by a formula. In this case the number stored is simply too long for the cell width.

A20	↓		'(5)		
	A	**B**	**C**	**D**	**D**
20	(5)				
21		100	1000	#NUM!	=B21^C21
22		16		#NUM!	=SQRT(-B22)
23					
24	(6)				
25		Text	50	#VALUE!	=B25/C25
26					
27	(7)				
28				########	100000000
29					
30	(8)				
31		100			
32			50	2	=B31/C32

(8) **#REF!** To generate this error requires another stage.

It was seen (on the previous page) that the original formula divided the content of cell B31 by the content of cell C32, initially producing the correct answer.

1 Row 31 is selected by clicking its heading.

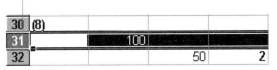

2 From the Edit menu the command Delete is selected to delete the whole row.

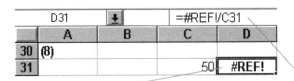

3 Since the cell previously referred to as B31 has been deleted, the error message is displayed because the Reference to the cell is no longer valid.

4 Note on the formula bar that the formula has been changed so that the B31 reference is replaced by #REF! and that the C32 reference is updated to C31.

These examples have been contrived deliberately to give simple practical examples of what causes the error values. In practice this is not usually as obvious because a single error may cause a proliferation of error values.

Auting Tools

The Auditing features are available in the following ways:

HANDY TIP

Auditing displays tracer arrows between cells. In order to make these arrows more visible, it is better to remove the grid lines. To do this, select Options from the Tools menu and on the View tab uncheck the Gridlines option.

(a)   Clicking Auditing from the Tools menu.

(b)   From the Auditing toolbar. To display the Auditing toolbar, check Show Auditing Toolbar in the Auditing sub-menu.

Inserting Precedent Tracers

Precedents are the cells referred to in the formula of the selected cell.

Select the cell which contains a formula with references to other cells, i.e. Precedents.

HANDY TIP

The Trace Precedents button can be clicked a number of times to display the next level of cell precedents. When no more levels exist, a beep will be heard.

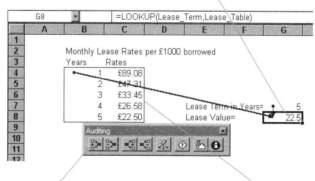

2   On the Auditing toolbar, click the Trace Precedents button.

3   Note the arrows from the precedent cell and the box around the table.

Inserting Dependent Tracers

Dependents are the cells that contain formulas which refer to the selected cell.

To remove the whole set of tracer arrows on the worksheet, e.g. to finish the audit or perhaps to recommence from a different cell, simply click the Remove All Arrows button.

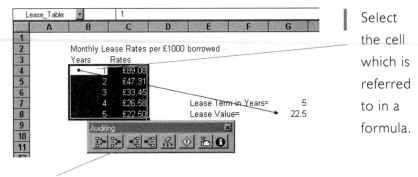

Select the cell which is referred to in a formula.

2 Click the Trace Dependents button once for each level.

3 Note the arrow from the selected cell to the cell containing the formula.

Navigating Tracer Arrows

To change the selected cell by moving within the interconnecting network of tracer arrows:

1 Point to the tracer arrow so that the pointer cross changes to an arrow.

2 Double-click the left mouse button.

Using the Error Tracer

1 Select the last cell which contains an error value.

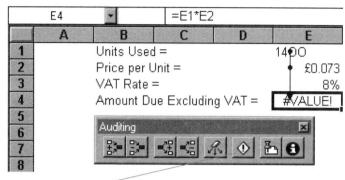

Trace Error locates all the cells affected by the original error, but it makes active the cell which contains the first occurrence.

2 Click the Trace Error button.

3 The error is traced back to cells E1 and E2. It can be seen that cell E1 contains '14OO', i.e. the digits 1 and 4 followed by two capital 'O's instead of '1400'.

4 Select cell E1 and key in '1400'.

Always clear existing tracer arrows before reusing Trace Error.

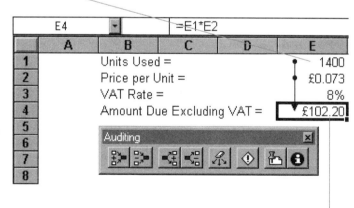

5 The error value in E4 is replaced by the correct result.

Using Cell Notes

You may attach notes to cells to provide some explanation to the worksheet.

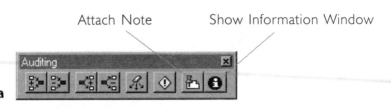

Attach Note   Show Information Window

HANDY TIP

To delete a note from a cell, select the cell and note from the Notes in Sheet list and click the Delete button.

Adding a Note to a Cell

1 Select the cell.

2 Click the Attach Note button on the Auditing toolbar.

3 Enter the note in the Text Note box.

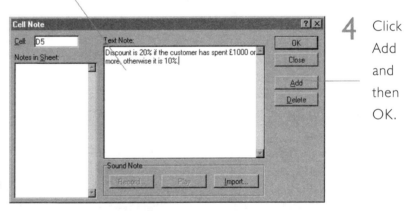

4 Click Add and then OK.

HANDY TIP

If no red dot is displayed in the top right-hand corner of a cell, from the Tools menu click Options and check the Note Indicator box on the View tab.

To Read a Cell Note

Cells with notes have a small red dot in the top right-hand corner. Point to the cell and the cell note will automatically be displayed.

Alternatively, select the cell and click the Display Info button on the Auditing toolbar. The Information window can be closed just like any other window.

CHAPTER EIGHT

Workbook and Worksheet Security

Excel provides a variety of security options to protect workbooks and worksheets from being corrupted.

Covers

Protecting Workbook Files

Workbook files can be protected by adding a password to the file to prevent unauthorised personnel from gaining access.

Creating a Password

REMEMBER

Rules for passwords: The maximum length allowed is 15 characters. They can be any combination of letters, digits and other symbols. They are case-sensitive.

1 Click Save As from the File menu.

2 Click Options.

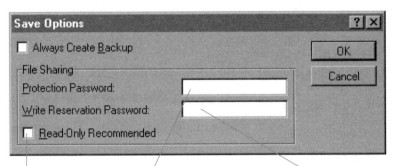

3 Protection Password – will be supplied to users to allow them to open the file and access the data but will not allow them to save changes under the existing filename.

4 Write Reservation Password will be supplied to users who are allowed to change the existing file.

BEWARE

If you lose or forget the password, the file cannot be recovered.

5 The Read-Only Recommended box is checked to issue a warning to dissuade users from changing the existing file unless absolutely necessary.

6 Confirmation of both passwords will be requested.

...contd

Opening a Password-protected File

1 Click Save As from the File Menu.

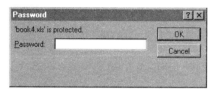

2 After entering the filename, you will be asked for the Protection Password.

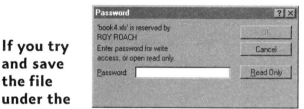

3 After entering the correct Protection Password, another Password dialogue box will be displayed.

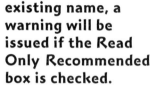

If you try and save the file under the existing name, a warning will be issued if the Read Only Recommended box is checked.

4 If you wish to change the existing file, key in the Write Reservation Password, otherwise click the Read Only button.

Removal of Password Protection

1 Click Open from the File menu.

2 Key in both the Protection and the Write Reservation passwords.

3 Click Save As from the File menu.

4 Click the Options button and delete both passwords.

5 Uncheck the Read Only Recommended box, if crossed.

6 Complete Save As dialogue box for existing filename.

Protecting Workbook Structure

It is possible to protect the structure of the workbook, i.e. the order, number and names of sheets and the arrangement of the windows.

1   Click Protection from the Tools menu.

2   Click Protect Workbook from the Protection sub-menu.

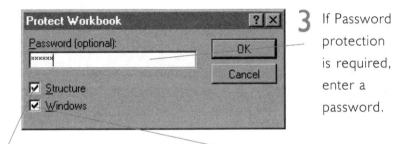

3   If Password protection is required, enter a password.

To remove protection, click Protection from the Options menu and then select the Unprotect Workbook option.

4   If Structure protection is required, check the box.

5   If Windows protection is required, check the box.

6   If a password is entered, you will be requested to confirm it by re-keying it.

When protection is applied, certain commands are 'greyed out':

Edit menu – Delete Sheet, Move or Copy Sheet.

Format menu – the Sheet sub-menu commands, Rename, Hide and Unhide.

Also, the Minimise and Maximise icons and the Control menu box on the Command menu bar and the Window Sizing borders are hidden.

Protecting Workbook Sheets

Cells may be protected so that their contents are not overwritten. This works in the following way:

- Unlock the cells which can be changed.

Normally by default, all cells in a worksheet will be locked so that once the sheet is protected, no changes can be made to any cells.

- Activate Sheet Protection.

1 Select the range of cells you want to unlock.

2 Click Cells from the Format menu.

3 In the Format Cells dialogue box, click the Protection tab.

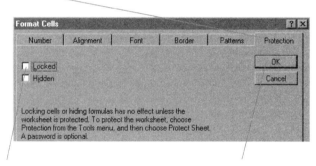

If the Hidden box is checked, the formula(s) in the cell(s) will be hidden.

4 Uncheck Locked.

5 Click OK.

6 Click Protection from the Tools menu and then select Protect Sheet.

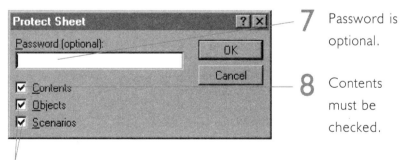

7 Password is optional.

8 Contents must be checked.

9 Objects and Scenarios would normally be checked.

The Effects of Cell Protection

1   If you attempt to overwrite or edit a cell which is locked, then an error message is issued.

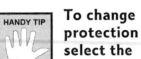

To change protection select the cells, unprotect Sheet, then from the Format Cells Protection tab, uncheck or check Locked as required and click OK.

2   When a locked cell is selected, certain commands on the Command menu bar will be 'greyed out'.

3   If you press the Tab key, then the selected cell will change to the next Unlocked cell, following the order from top to bottom and from left to right. Pressing Shift + Tab will reverse the order. This is a very efficient way of locating unlocked cells.

CHAPTER NINE

What-If Tests

The basis of What-If testing is changing the value of numeric data in cells and investigating the effect on dependent formulas. Basic What-If tests were introduced in Chapter Two. In addition to these, Excel provides more sophisticated techniques of What-If analysis which will be described in this chapter.

Covers

An Overview

To illustrate some of the techniques of What-If analysis, the following example of Video Rentals will be used.

	A	B	C	D	E
1					
2		**Video Rentals**			
3					
4		Rental Price =		£2.00	
5		Number of Rentals =		250	
6		Total Income =		£500.00	
7					
8		Total Costs =		£200.00	
9					
10		Net Profit =		£300.00	
11					

Total Income is calculated as
Rental Price x Number of Rentals.

Net Profit is calculated as
Total Income – Total Costs.

The chapter looks at various techniques which show how the Net Profit relates to the Number of Rentals and the Rental Price.

Automatic Versus Manual Calculation

By default, Excel automatically recalculates formulas in dependent cells when the values in precedent cells are changed. Usually this occurs so fast that there is no noticeable delay, though if the network of dependent formulas is large and complex there may be some delay. It can prove particularly frustrating if you wish to change several values and are made to wait after each one whilst the rest of the worksheet is recalculated. In such cases it is better to switch to Manual Calculation.

REMEMBER

You must return to this dialogue box or press F9 every time you require a recalculation.

1 Click Options from the Tools menu.

2 Click the Calculation tab.

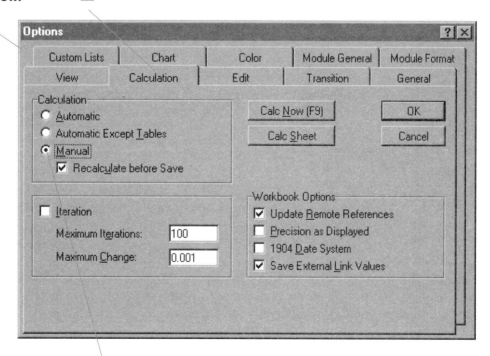

3 Check the Manual option. The option of recalculating before Save is now available.

Goal Seek Command

Suppose, in the Video Rental example, we wanted to know the number of rentals necessary to break even, i.e. to cover the total costs so that the net profit is £0. To do this you would use a Goal Seek What-If test:

1 Select the cell Net_Profit which contains the formula Total_Income – Total_Costs.

2 Click Goal Seek from the Tools menu.

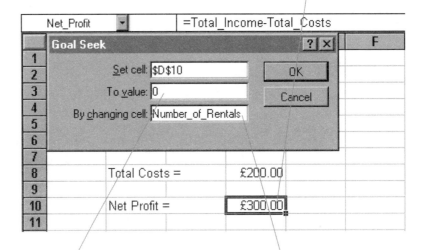

3 Key in the target value in the Goal Seek dialogue box.

4 Key in the changing cell reference in the Goal Seek dialogue box.

5 Goal Seek finds that 100 rentals reduces the
Net Profit to £0.

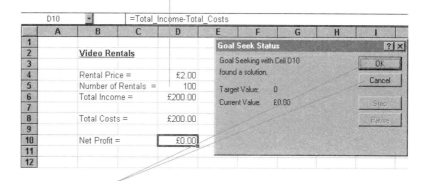

6 Click OK to confirm changes to the worksheet, or
click Cancel to restore previous values.

One-Input Data Tables

Suppose, in the Video Rental example, we wanted to know how the Net Profit would change when the Rental Price is changed. We could do this using the simple What-If technique of varying the Rental Price and recording the corresponding change in the Net Profit. However this is more easily done by using a one-input data table:

Select cell G3. Note that this position above the second column is critical.

	G3	▾						
	A	B	C	D	E	F	G	H
1								
2		Video Rentals				Rental Price	Net Profit	
3								
4		Rental Price =		£2.00		£1.00		
5		Number of Rentals =		250		£1.25		
6		Total Income =		£500.00		£1.50		
7						£1.75		
8		Total Costs =		£200.00		£2.00		
9						£2.25		
10		Net Profit =		£300.00		£2.50		
11								

2 In cell G3, key in the formula which calculates the Net Profit. In this case, simply refer to the value of the cell, i.e. enter '= Net_Profit' or '=D10'.

...contd

3 Select the table as shown below. This is critical and must include cell G3 and both columns.

4 Click Table from the Data menu.

	A	B	C	D	E	F	G	H
1								
2		Table			? X	Rental Price	Net Profit	
3		Row Input Cell:			OK		£300.00	
4		Column Input Cell:	Rental_Price	Cancel		£1.00		
5						£1.25		
6						£1.50		
7						£1.75		
8		Total Costs =	£200.00			£2.00		
9						£2.25		
10		Net Profit =	£300.00			£2.50		
11								

5 Complete the Table dialogue box. Since a one-input vertical table is required, it is only necessary to complete the Column Input cell. This is the cell reference into which the left hand column values are to be substituted, i.e. Rental_Price.

6 Clicking OK will produce this table.

Rental Price	Net Profit
	£300.00
£1.00	£50.00
£1.25	£112.50
£1.50	£175.00
£1.75	£237.50
£2.00	£300.00
£2.25	£362.50
£2.50	£425.00

Two-Input Data Tables

Suppose, in the Video Rental example, we wanted to know how the Net Profit would vary relative to the Rental Price and also to the Number of Rentals. A two-input data table could be used as shown below:

1 Select the cell at the intersection of the row containing the first input value (Number_of_Rentals) and the second input value (Rental_Price).

2 Key in the formula which calculates the Net Profit. In this case, simply refer to the value of the cell, i.e. enter '= Net_Profit' or '=D10'.

E	F	G	H	I	J	K	L
	Rental Price	Net Profit					
		Number of Rentals					
	£300.00	100	125	150	175	200	
	£1.00						
	£1.25						
	£1.50						
	£1.75						
	£2.00						
	£2.25						
	£2.50						

3 Select the table as shown. This selection is critical: it must include the cell at the intersection, the column and row of input data and the empty body of the table.

...contd

4 Click Table from the Data menu.

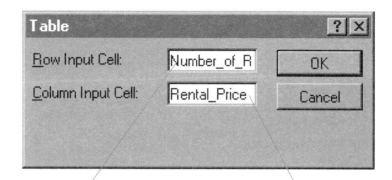

5 For the row input cell, enter Number_of Rentals.

6 For the column input cell, enter Rental_Price.

7 Click OK to produce the table below.

Rental Price	Net Profit				
	Number of Rentals				
£300.00	100	125	150	175	200
£1.00	-£100.00	-£75.00	-£50.00	-£25.00	£0.00
£1.25	-£75.00	-£43.75	-£12.50	£18.75	£50.00
£1.50	-£50.00	-£12.50	£25.00	£62.50	£100.00
£1.75	-£25.00	£18.75	£62.50	£106.25	£150.00
£2.00	£0.00	£50.00	£100.00	£150.00	£200.00
£2.25	£25.00	£81.25	£137.50	£193.75	£250.00
£2.50	£50.00	£112.50	£175.00	£237.50	£300.00

The table is calculated rapidly and shows at a glance the relationship between rental price and number of rentals.

What-If Scenarios

What is a Scenario?

A scenario is a set of What-If precedent cell references and their input values, which you can name for subsequent recall. This enables sets of input values to be changed very quickly in What-If tests and saves having to record them and rekey them each time they are required.

These techniques are available by using the Tools menu Scenarios option or by using the Scenarios box on the Workgroup toolbar.

Adding Scenarios using the Scenarios Box

Suppose in the Video Rental example, we require to set up two sets of input values representing the Best Case and the Worse Case. The input values are Rental_Price, Number_of_Rentals and Total_Costs. The procedure for adding a scenario is as follows:

1 Key in the values required. In this case the Best Case values are £2.50, 200 and £100 for the Rental_Price, Number_of_Rentals and Total_Costs respectively.

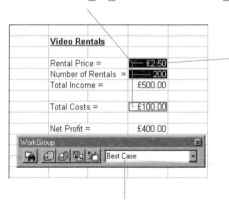

2 Select all input values, by clicking the first and then holding down the Ctrl key while you click the remainder.

3 Key in the name of the scenario, 'Best Case' in the Scenario Box.

4 Key in the values required for the Worst Case: £1.00 for the Rental_Price, 250 for the Number_of_Rentals and £125 for Total_Costs and select the values as before.

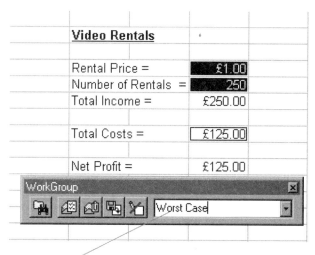

Scenario values can be changed by entering new values and then reselecting the Scenario name.

5 Overtype the scenario name with the new name 'Worst Case'.

Displaying Scenario Values using the Scenario Box

1 Click the arrow to the right of the Scenario box.

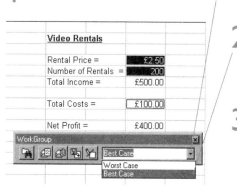

2 Click the scenario name required from the list.

3 The input cells will be altered to the scenario values and the changes will ripple through the worksheet.

...contd

Using the Scenario Manager Dialogue Box

1 From the Tools menu, select the Scenario option.

2 Complete the following dialogue box:

Click the Show button to display the scenario values in the input cells.

Select the Name of the required scenario.

Click the Close button when you have finished.

Click the Add button to add another scenario.

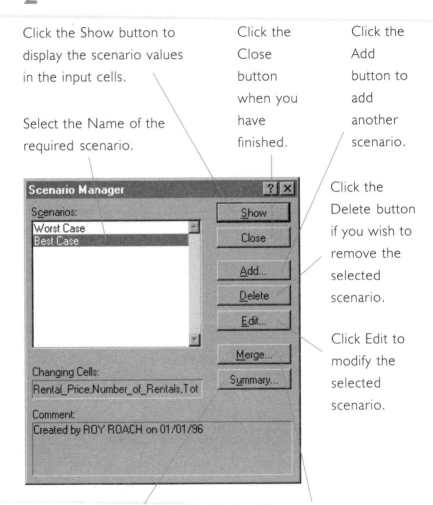

Click the Delete button if you wish to remove the selected scenario.

Click Edit to modify the selected scenario.

Click the Summary button to produce a report on the scenarios.

Click the Merge button to merge a scenario from another worksheet or workbook.

CHAPTER TEN

Multiple Worksheets and Workbooks

A workbook file can contain multiple worksheets allowing data to be subdivided into smaller units, thereby avoiding complex and cumbersome worksheets. Alternatively it is possible for data to be subdivided into different workbooks which may be linked.

Covers

Using Multiple Worksheets

Renaming A Worksheet

Rather than accepting the default names, it is better to give worksheets more meaningful names.

Point to the worksheet tab.

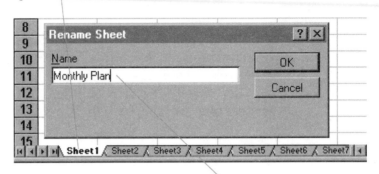

2 Double-click the left mouse button.

3 In the Rename Sheet dialogue box, enter the new name.

4 Click OK.

Moving Sheets within a Workbook

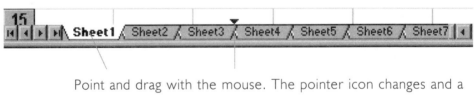

Point and drag with the mouse. The pointer icon changes and a small insertion marker appears.

Moving Sheets Between Workbooks

| Click the Move or Copy Sheet option from the Edit menu.

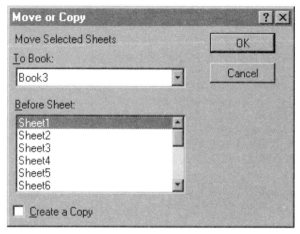

2 Select the destination workbook, which must be open.

3 Select the new location within the workbook.

4 Check the box to copy, uncheck to move.

Inserting a Worksheet

| Select the sheet that occupies the position for the new sheet.

2 Click the Worksheet option from the Insert menu.

Deleting a Worksheet

| Select the sheet to be deleted.

2 Click the Delete Sheet option from the Edit menu.

3 A warning dialogue box will be displayed. Click OK if you are absolutely sure. You cannot undo this command.

Viewing Several Worksheets

It is possible to view several worksheets and/or workbooks simultaneously. This can be particularly useful when they are linked via common data.

Opening Extra Windows

To view more than one worksheet, it is necessary first to open another window.

To switch active sheets, either select from the Window menu or click on the window of a sheet.

| 1 | Suppose Sheet 1 of Book 3 is made active by clicking its tab. |

| 2 | Click New Window from the Window menu. |

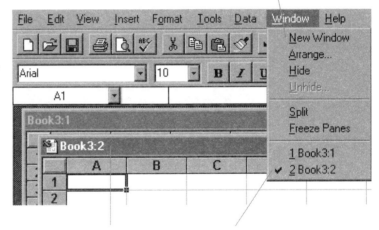

A window can be closed by clicking in the Control panel on the top right-hand corner.

| 3 | An extra window is displayed for Sheet 2. This is now the active sheet. |

...contd

The Windows Arrange Command

Click Arrange from the Windows menu.

Tiled will display the windows side by side.

Horizontal will produce a column of tiles, i.e. with horizontal subdivisions.

To revert to viewing one window, make the window active and click its maximise button.

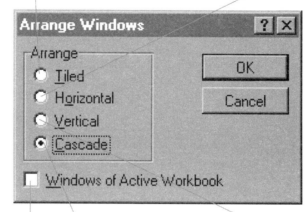

To size windows, point to the border and drag.

Cascade will overlay the windows with a slight offset.

Vertical will produce a row of tiles, i.e. with vertical subdivisions.

Check this if you wish to restrict display to the active workbook and its windows.

To move windows, point to the Title bar and drag.

Links Within Workbooks

Consider the following example where sales figures for 1992 and sales figures for 1993 are contained on separate worksheets. A third worksheet contains a summary of 1992 and 1993.

	A	B	C	D	E
1		Sales Figures 1992			
2		Qtr1	Qtr2	Qtr3	Qtr4
3		£9,000	£11,000	£17,000	£13,000

	A	B	C	D	E
1		Sales Figures 1993			
2		Qtr1	Qtr2	Qtr3	Qtr4
3		£10,000	£12,000	£19,000	£14,000

	A	B	C	D
1		Summary 1992-1993		
2				
3	Qtr1	£19,000		
4	Qtr2	£23,000		
5	Qtr3	£36,000		
6	Qtr4	£27,000		
7	Total	£105,000		
8				

...contd

1 Select the cell where the answer is to go. E.g., B3 on the Summary sheet.

2 Press '=' to start formula.

3 Click the tab of the Sales 1992 sheet. This will become the active sheet.

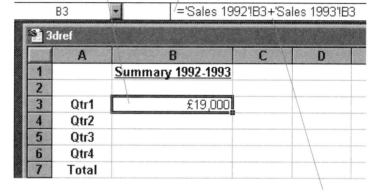

HANDY TIP

Links can also be formed by selecting cell names from the Name box. The Name box contains a list of names which have been defined for the whole workbook and are available in all worksheets. These are referred to as 'Book Level' names.

4 Click cell B3 on the Sales 1992 sheet. The formula on the formula bar will be shown as ='Sales 1992'!B3.

5 Press '+'.

6 Click the tab of the Sales 1993 sheet. This will become the active sheet.

7 Click cell B3 on the Sales 1993 sheet. The formula on the formula bar will be shown as ='Sales 1992'!B3+'Sales 1993'!B3.

8 Press Enter. The answer is displayed on the Summary sheet.

3D References

In the example on the previous page, all the worksheets have exactly the same format in that each quarterly amount lies in the same cell on each sheet. It is useful to picture the sheets as a set of layers with identical layouts.

An alternative method of summarising the sales figures on the third sheet is to use a 3D reference.

To enter a 3D reference, you can key it in, but it is much easier to point and click.

1 Select the cell where the answer is to go.

B3	▼	=SUM('Sales 1992:Sales 1993'!B3)

3dref

	A	B
1		**Summary 1992-1993**
2		
3	Qtr1	=SUM('Sales 1992:Sales 1993'!B3)
4	Qtr2	=SUM('Sales 1992:Sales 1993'!C3)
5	Qtr3	=SUM('Sales 1992:Sales 1993'!D3)
6	Qtr4	=SUM('Sales 1992:Sales 1993'!E3)
7	Total	=SUM(B3:B6)

2 Enter '=SUM' to start the formula.

3 Click the tab of the first sheet. Excel inserts 'Sales 1992'

4 Press the Shift key for a range of adjacent sheets and click the tab of the last sheet so that Excel extends the reference to 'Sales 1992:Sales 1993'.

5 Click the cell or range of cells that is the same for all sheets, e.g. B3, and Excel will complete the reference 'Sales 1992:Sales 1993'!B3.

Links between Workbooks

To illustrate how links can be formed between workbooks, a new example of quarterly sales over three years will be used:

1 Suppose the data shown below was keyed into a worksheet named 'Annual Summary' in a workbook file named '91_SALES.XLS'. It can be seen that the four selected cells containing the quarterly sales figures were named 'Qtrly_Sales'.

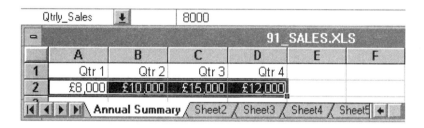

2 Correspondingly, the sales figures were keyed into exactly similar locations named 'Qtrly_Sales' in worksheets named 'Annual Summary' in new workbook files named '92_SALES.XLS' and '93_SALES.XLS' respectively.

3 The first workbook, '91_SALES.XLS', was then closed, the file being saved on the hard disk in the directory specified by the path 'C:\MY DOCUMENTS'.

...contd

4 In the workbook '93_SALES.XLS', a second worksheet was named 'Three Year Summary' and was used to record the total sales figures for the three years, as shown below.

5 In '93_SALES.XLS', a second window was opened to display its second worksheet. The Window menu showed the three windows available. A tiled display of these three windows is shown below and a display of the formulas used, giving the links specifications, is shown on the opposite page.

92_SALES.XLS

	A	B	C	D	E	F
1	Qtr 1	Qtr 2	Qtr 3	Qtr 4		
2	£9,000	£11,000	£17,000	£13,000		

Annual Summary / Sheet2 / Sheet3 / Sheet4 / Sheet5 / She

93_SALES.XLS:1

	A	B	C	D	E	F
1	Qtr 1	Qtr 2	Qtr 3	Qtr 4		
2	£10,000	£12,000	£19,000	£14,000		

Annual Summary / Three Year Summary / Sheet3 / Sheet4

93_SALES.XLS:2

	A	B	C	D	E
1		Annual Totals			
2	1991:	£45,000			
3	1992:	£50,000			
4	1993:	£55,000			
5					
6	Three Year Total:	£150,000			

Annual Summary \ **Three Year Summary** / Sheet3 / S

...contd

	A	B
		Annual Totals
1		
2	1991:	=SUM('C:\EXCEL_5\EXAMPLES\91_SALES.XLS'!Qtrly_Sales)
3	1992:	=SUM('92_SALES.XLS'!Qtrly_Sales)
4	1993:	=SUM(Qtrly_Sales)
5		
6	Three Year Total:	=SUM(B2:B4)

93_SALES.XLS:2

Tabs: Annual Summary / **Three Year Summary** / Sheet3 / S

Cell B2: Since the workbook is closed, the full path for its file must be specified to enable Excel to locate it.

HANDY TIP

To insert in a formula the specification for a link to another workbook: Assuming that the workbook is open, use the Window menu to display the workbook, click worksheet tab and either select the cell(s) or use the Name box to select the name. If the workbook is closed, you will have to key in the full specification, including the path.

Cell B3: Since the file is open, it is necessary to specify only the workbook filename and the cell's name.

Cell B4: Since the link is to a worksheet in the same workbook, it is necessary to give only the name of the cells, because this is a Book-Level name.

Hiding Rows and Columns using 'Hide' Command

If a worksheet contains a mass of information, it is possible to temporarily hide some of the data to get a clearer overview on the screen.

1. Select the rows or columns to be hidden, e.g. in this case the two ranges, rows 13:17 and rows 24:30.

2. Click Row or Column from the Format menu and then click Hide.

3. The resulting screen will show the main features of the data.

	A	B	C	D	E	F	G	H	I
6				January	February	March	April	May	June
7									
8	FILMS PER MONTH =			1632	576	768	1152	1344	1920
9									
10	SALES INCOME =			£6,250.21	£2,205.96	£2,941.28	£4,411.91	£5,147.23	£7,353.19
11									
12	SALES COSTS								
18		TOTAL =		£3,750.07	£2,482.87	£2,713.27	£3,174.07	£3,404.47	£4,095.67
19									
20	GROSS PROFIT =			£2,500.15	-£276.91	£228.01	£1,237.85	£1,742.77	£3,257.52
21	% GROSS PROFIT =			40.0%	-12.6%	7.8%	28.1%	33.9%	44.3%
22									
23	EXPENSES								
31		TOTAL =		£1,616.67	£1,616.67	£1,616.67	£1,616.67	£1,616.67	£1,616.67
32									
33	NET PROFIT =			£883.48	-£1,893.58	-£1,388.66	-£378.82	£126.10	£1,640.86
34	% NET PROFIT =			14.1%	-85.8%	-47.2%	-8.6%	2.4%	22.3%
35									

Scenario Summary / Monthly Plan \ **Annual Plan** / Sh

HANDY TIP

To unhide all rows and/or columns, click the Select All button first.

1. Make a selection containing the hidden rows or columns.

2. Click Row or Column from Format menu and then click Unhide.

Hiding Rows and Columns using 'Outlining'

An alternative method of hiding rows or columns is to use outlining.

1 Make SEPARATE selections of the rows or columns to be hidden, e.g. in this case first the range of rows 13:17 and later the range of rows 24:30.

2 Click Group and Outline from the Data menu and then click Group.

3 The resulting screen will show the Outline Row Level Bar. Click the Hide Detail Symbol (–) or the Show Detail Symbol (+) to control the data on the display.

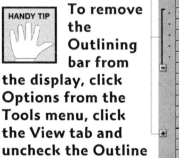

HANDY TIP To remove the Outlining bar from the display, click Options from the Tools menu, click the View tab and uncheck the Outline Symbols box.

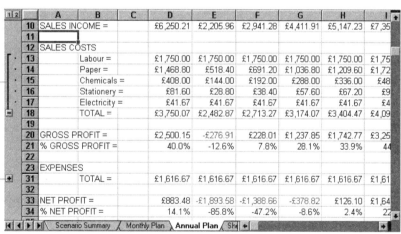

	A	B	C	D	E	F	G	H	I
10	SALES INCOME =			£6,250.21	£2,205.96	£2,941.28	£4,411.91	£5,147.23	£7,35
11									
12	SALES COSTS								
13		Labour =		£1,750.00	£1,750.00	£1,750.00	£1,750.00	£1,750.00	£1,75
14		Paper =		£1,468.80	£518.40	£691.20	£1,036.80	£1,209.60	£1,72
15		Chemicals =		£408.00	£144.00	£192.00	£288.00	£336.00	£48
16		Stationery =		£81.60	£28.80	£38.40	£57.60	£67.20	£9
17		Electricity =		£41.67	£41.67	£41.67	£41.67	£41.67	£4
18		TOTAL =		£3,750.07	£2,482.87	£2,713.27	£3,174.07	£3,404.47	£4,09
19									
20	GROSS PROFIT =			£2,500.15	-£276.91	£228.01	£1,237.85	£1,742.77	£3,25
21	% GROSS PROFIT =			40.0%	-12.6%	7.8%	28.1%	33.9%	44
22									
23	EXPENSES								
31		TOTAL =		£1,616.67	£1,616.67	£1,616.67	£1,616.67	£1,616.67	£1,61
32									
33	NET PROFIT =			£883.48	-£1,893.58	-£1,388.66	-£378.82	£126.10	£1,64
34	% NET PROFIT =			14.1%	-85.8%	-47.2%	-8.6%	2.4%	22

Scenario Summary / Monthly Plan \ **Annual Plan** / Sh

Removing an Outline

1 Make a selection containing the outlined rows or columns.

2 Click Group and Outline from the Data menu and then click Clear Outline.

Using Window Split and Freeze Panes

If a worksheet is very wide, it helps if the screen is split vertically, so that the row labels are separated from the numerical data. Furthermore, the left-hand pane can be frozen so that data isn't accidentally scrolled. In the following example the screen is split vertically between columns C and D.

HANDY TIP

The screen can also be split horizontally by selecting the row where the split is required or by dragging the Horizontal Split bar.

1 Split the screen vertically by dragging the Vertical Split box to the boundary between columns C and D.

or

Select column D and click Split from the Window menu.

2 Select cell on left-hand side and click Freeze Panes from the Window menu.

	A	B	C	K	L	M	N	O	P
6				August	September	October	November	December	Totals
7									
8	FILMS PER MONTH =			2880	2496	1824	1344	960	19200
9									
10	SALES INCOME =			£11,029.79	£9,559.15	£6,985.53	£5,147.23	£3,676.60	£73,531.91
11									
12	SALES COSTS								
18	TOTAL =			£5,247.67	£4,786.87	£3,980.47	£3,404.47	£2,943.67	£44,540.00
19									
20	GROSS PROFIT =			£5,782.12	£4,772.28	£3,005.07	£1,742.77	£732.93	£28,991.91
21	% GROSS PROFIT =			52.4%	49.9%	43.0%	33.9%	19.9%	39.4%
22									
23	EXPENSES								
31	TOTAL =			£1,616.67	£1,616.67	£1,616.67	£1,616.67	£1,616.67	£19,400.00
32									
33	NET PROFIT =			£4,165.45	£3,155.62	£1,388.40	£126.10	-£883.74	£9,591.91
34	% NET PROFIT =			37.8%	33.0%	19.9%	2.4%	-24.0%	13.0%
35									

Scenario Summary / Monthly Plan \ Annual Plan / Sh

HANDY TIP

Alternatively, double-click the Split bar to remove the Window Split.

The left pane is frozen; it has no scroll bars. The right pane can be scrolled horizontally to pan across the whole width of data.

Removing Freeze Panes and Window Split

1 Click Unfreeze Panes from the Window menu.

2 Click Remove Split from the Window menu.

CHAPTER ELEVEN

Formatting Worksheets

Once you have typed in your data and created formulas, you will be ready to improve the presentation of your worksheet before printing it. Excel provides extensive formatting facilities to enable you to do this.

Covers

Format Menu/Formatting Toolbar

To format cells, you have a choice of using the Format Command menu or the Formatting toolbar. As usual the Command menu gives you the widest range of choices but the selection of facilities packed into the toolbar will enable you to apply the majority of formats required.

The Cells... command displays the Format Cells dialogue box, which gives access to the tabs shown above.

 Select the cell(s) to be formatted and then choose the command from the menu or click the appropriate icon on the toolbar.

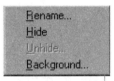

The Row sub-menu gives access to the row height and Hide/Unhide commands.

The AutoFormat and Style dialogue boxes will be dealt with in subsequent sections.

The Column sub-menu gives access to the column width and Hide/Unhide commands.

The Sheet sub-menu gives access to the Rename, Background and Hide/Unhide commands.

The Formatting Toolbar

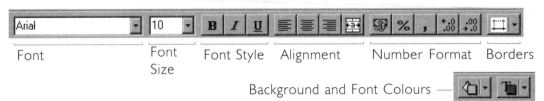

Font — Font Size — Font Style — Alignment — Number Format — Borders

Background and Font Colours —

Using AutoFormat

The AutoFormat command is designed to be used for tables.

1 | Select the area which requires formatting.

2 | From the Format menu, select the AutoFormat option.

3 | In the AutoFormat dialogue box you may try various Table formats until the Sample is acceptable.

HANDY TIP

If Excel fails to locate a Table format from your selection, an appropriate warning message will be displayed.

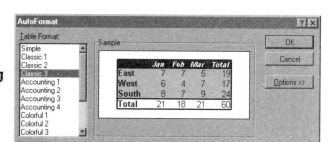

HANDY TIP

Even if you find that the Table formats supplied for AutoFormat are not acceptable to you, they will give you some ideas of the different types of appearance that can be applied to your data. It is also useful to view some of the workbooks supplied with Excel.

4 | Click Options and the following is displayed. By unchecking the check boxes, you can suppress some formats and see the effect in the sample box.

5 | Click OK to format your selection.

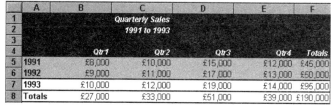

6 | If you are unhappy with the results, then you can restore your original selection by selecting the Undo AutoFormat option from the Edit menu.

Alignment and Orientation

The Formatting toolbar provides control only of horizontal alignment. For vertical alignment, fill, orientation, text wrap and justification, you must use the Alignment tab of the Format Cells dialogue box.

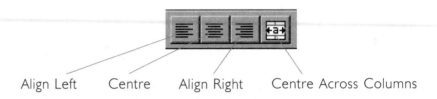

Align Left   Centre   Align Right   Centre Across Columns

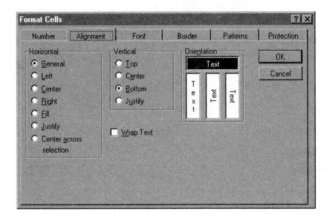

General means left for text and right for numbers.

Fill means to repeat character(s) across the width of cell.

Justify means to wrap text and to increase inter-word gaps to give alignment to the right as well as the left.

Centre across selection means centre the contents of the left-hand cell of the selection across the width of the selection.

Vertical Justify means to wrap the text and to increase the inter-line gaps (leading) so that the lines of text fill the row height.

Wrap Text can be applied to both horizontal and vertical alignment. It constrains the text to the width of the cell, splitting it into lines. The height of the containing row is adjusted automatically to accommodate the extra lines.

Fonts and Sizes

The Formatting toolbar provides a substantial degree of control over Fonts, Font Sizes, Font Styles and Font Colour via the lists and the Colour palette. However for some additional features such as subscripts and superscripts, it is necessary to use the Font tab on the Format Cells dialogue box.

HANDY TIP

**Try using as a toggle the keyboard shortcuts:
Ctrl+B for Bold
Ctrl+I for Italic
Ctrl+U for Underline.**

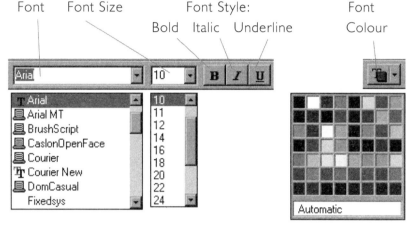

Font   Font Size   Font Style:
Bold Italic Underline

Font Colour

HANDY TIP

To format individual characters, go into edit mode, either on the formula bar or directly at the cell. Select the character(s) to be formatted by clicking and dragging the mouse. Then apply the format required using the Format menu or the Formatting toolbar.

1 Select the cells you wish to apply the font to.

2 Click Cells from the Format menu and click the Font tab.

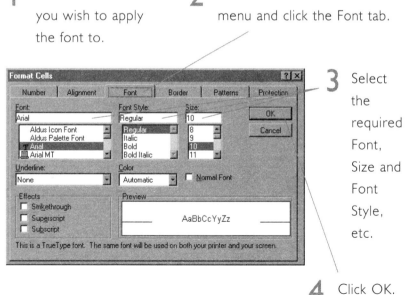

3 Select the required Font, Size and Font Style, etc.

4 Click OK.

Cell Borders

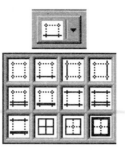

The Formatting toolbar provides a substantial choice of borders but for the full range of options you have to use the Border tab in the Format Cells dialogue box.

HANDY TIP

You may find it easier to remove the cell gridlines before setting borders so you can see where the border is. To do this select Tools, Options and on the View tab uncheck the gridlines box.

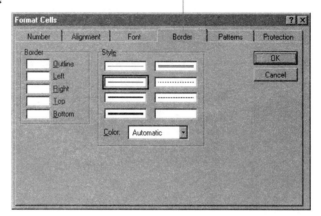

To achieve the effect shown in the example below, carry out the following.

HANDY TIP

To remove borders, select the required cells and from the Border tab in the Format dialogue box, deselect any borders and select blank style.

1 Select cells B4:E8 and set left border to a thin line.

2 Select cells B4:F4, A8:F8, A5:A8, F4:F8 in turn and set outline border to a medium line.

	A	B	C	D	E	F
3						
4		Qtr1	Qtr2	Qtr3	Qtr4	Totals
5	1991	£8,000	£10,000	£15,000	£12,000	£45,000
6	1992	£9,000	£11,000	£17,000	£13,000	£50,000
7	1993	£10,000	£12,000	£19,000	£14,000	£95,000
8	Totals	£27,000	£33,000	£51,000	£39,000	£190,000
9						

Background Colours

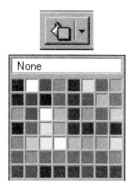

The Colour button on the Formatting toolbar gives access to the same colour palette as the Patterns tab of the Format Cells dialogue box, but is more convenient to use. You need only use the Patterns tab if you require the additional black-and-white patterns provided.

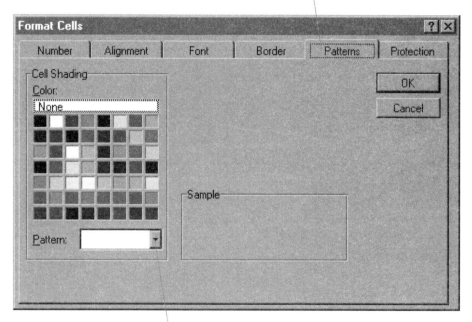

The Formatting toolbar colour palette is called a Tear-Off Palette since it can be moved by dragging its outline and can be left displayed for regular access.

Click here to display additional patterns.

Using the Format Painter

The Format Painter button is located on the standard toolbar, being placed in the Cut, Copy and Paste group. Its action is very powerful for copying the formats of cells.

Suppose, in the example below, you had experimented with the formatting for the cell C1, choosing 'Times New Roman' 16 point, Bold and Italic, Left Alignment with a grey background colour. You can save time setting up the format again for other cells.

HANDY TIP

The Format Painter can be kept active by double-clicking the Format Painter button with the formatted cell selected. The paintbrush icon will be attached to the pointer icon and will remain attached until the Format Painter button is clicked again.

1 Select the cell which contains the required format.

2 Click the Format Painter button. The 'paintbrush' icon will be attached to the pointer 'plus' icon.

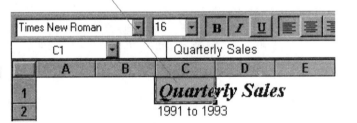

3 Select the cell or range of cells where the copied format is required, e.g. C1 to E2.

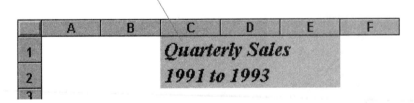

Number Formatting

The Formatting toolbar or the Number tab of the Format Cells dialogue box can be used to change the appearance of numbers and dates.

HANDY TIP

If the currency style does not appear as shown, you may have to adjust it. From the Format menu, select the Style... command. Select the Style name 'Currency'. Click the Modify button, select the Currency category and select a format.

Using the Formatting Toolbar

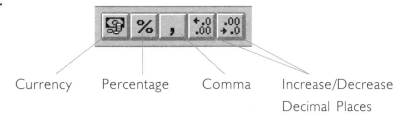

Currency   Percentage   Comma   Increase/Decrease Decimal Places

The example below illustrates this. Here the number '1250.7' was keyed in and stored in the body of the table. Initially it was displayed in the 'General Format', i.e. '1250.7'. The two-stage process was used to change the formats. The blank cells were left where it was not possible to reduce the decimal places.

		A	B	C	D	E	F	G	H
1									
2		(2) Second Adjust				(1) First Select Style:			
3		Decimal Places				General Format	Currency Style	Percentage Style	Comma Style
5		Decrease Twice:					£1,251		1,251
6		Decrease Once:				1251	£1,250.7		1,250.7
7		No Change:				1250.7	£1,250.70	125070%	1,250.70
8		Increase Once:				1250.70	£1,250.700	125070.0%	1,250.700
9		Increase Twice:				1250.700	£1,250.7000	125070.00%	1,250.7000

...contd

Using the Format Cells Number Tab

1 Select the cell(s) to be formatted.

2 Click the Cells option from the Format menu.

3 Click the Number tab.

4 Select Category as 'Number'.

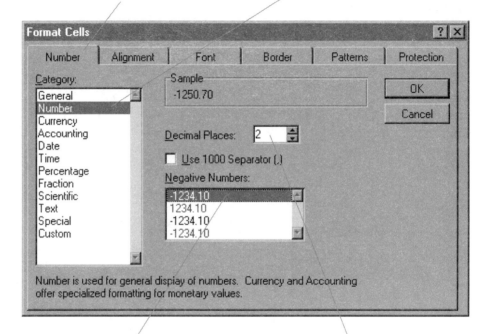

5 Select style.

6 Enter decimal places.

7 Click OK.

Customizing a Format Type

To customize a format type, either key in the new type in the Type box or edit an existing type using the Format Cells dialogue box.

| Select Category as Custom.

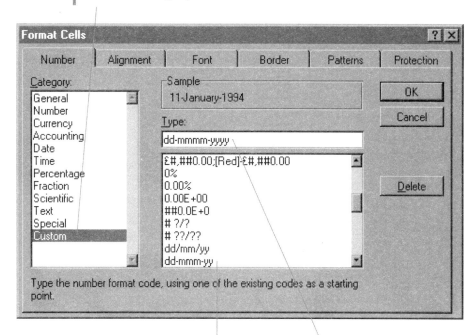

2 Select an existing type as a starting point.

3 Edit the existing type or enter a new type.

4 Click OK.

Removing a Custom Format Type

| Select the Format Type.

2 Click Delete.

Using Format Styles

It has been seen that considerable time and effort may be used in setting up the various combinations of formats for a spreadsheet. It is advantageous to store these specifications in 'Styles' which can be applied easily and quickly to selections of cells. This is similar to the style facility used in word processing and desk top publishing where combinations of formats are applied to paragraphs.

Keep the style simple! Select only single cells or cells which have identical formatting. Styles are not suitable for ranges of cells with different outline borders.

Creating New Styles

1 Select the formatted cell for which you wish to create the style.

2 Click the Style... option from the Format menu.

3 The Style dialogue box will be displayed.

Initially, the Style Name list box will contain only the default 'Normal' style and the 'Comma', 'Currency' and 'Percent' styles available on the Formatting toolbar.

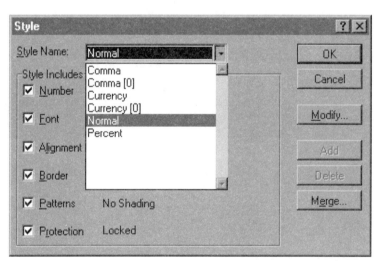

4 Key in the name of the new style. The Style dialogue box will list the format specification of the selected cell as shown on the next page.

Modify... Click to display the Format Cells dialogue box to define a new style or edit an existing one.

Style Includes: Check the boxes for the types of format to be included.

Add: After using the Format Cells dialogue box, click to add a new style.

Style Name: Key in new name.

Delete: If, subsequently, you wish to delete a custom style, select its name and click this button.

If you apply a style to previously formatted cells, the formatting of the newly applied style will override the original format.

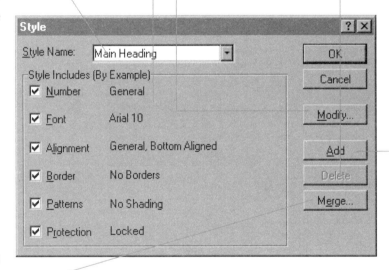

If you edit a style, then all cells previously formatted with that style name will have their formats updated.

Merge... Click to display the Merge dialogue box to enable styles to be copied from another open workbook.

Applying Styles

1 Select the cell or range of cells to be formatted.

2 Click the Style... command from the Format menu.

3 In the Style dialogue box, select the Style name required and click the OK key or press Enter.

The Edit Menu

Certain commands and sub-menus on the Edit menu are particularly relevant to formatting.

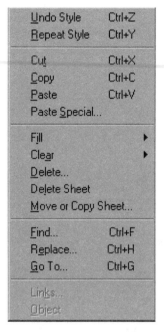

Repeat Style: If you have just used the Format Style command to apply a style to format cells, then the Repeat Style command becomes available. If you need to apply the same style to several ranges of cells, this can save you time in using the Style dialogue box and locating the style name.

Undo Style: Correspondingly, the Undo command becomes replaced by the Undo Style command.

Clear: The Clear sub-menu allows you to specify what is cleared from the selected cell(s), i.e. 'Contents', 'Formats', 'Notes' or 'All' three.

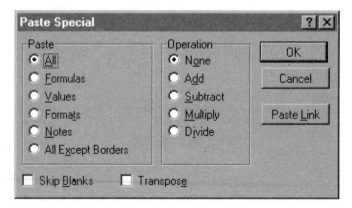

Paste Special... This is available when you have selected a cell and used the Copy (but not Cut) command. The dialogue box enables you to specify exactly what you want to paste from a cell range, e.g. 'Formats' only.

CHAPTER TWELVE

Printing Worksheets

Once you have completed your worksheet and formatted it, you will be ready to print it. This will involve subdividing long or wide spreadsheets into several pages, setting up the printed page and creating headers and footers.

Covers

Printing Commands

The usual sequence of commands to produce a quality printout would be Page Setup, followed by the introduction of manual page breaks, repeating row or column headings from page to page and finally adjusting the magnification of the printout to fit the page. After each change, the Print Preview facility would be used. Once the print preview is satisfactory, the Print command would be used to output to the printer.

Most of the commands are available from the File menu.

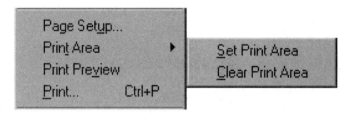

HANDY TIP

The Print Area can also be set from the Page tab in the Page Setup dialogue box.

The Page Break command is available from the Insert menu.

The Print Preview and the Print commands are available from the standard toolbar.

The Print button cuts out the Print dialogue box.   Print Preview   The Spell Checker button is part of this group.

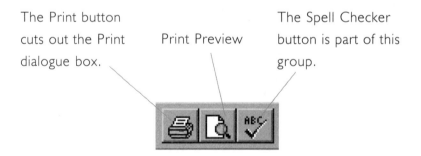

Setting Up the Printed Page

The Page and Sheet tabs from the Page Setup dialogue box will be described in this section.

| Click Page Setup from the File menu.

Orientation: Normally Portrait is required although for wide spreadsheets and charts Landscape is often used.

Print and Print Preview: Direct access to these commands. Print Preview allows you to test out page setup.

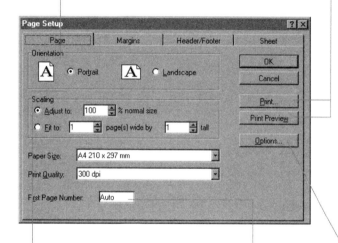

Scaling: *Either* Adjust to: (enter percentage size of worksheet to be fitted to the page); *or* Fit to: (enter number of pages you wish the worksheet to occupy).

Paper Size and Print Quality: Select from list.

Options: Displays a printer Options dialogue box.

First Page Number: Accept Auto or key in the starting page number if printout is to form part of a report.

...contd

2 Click Sheet tab.

Print Area: Although not strictly required, it's good practice to specify a cell range here as some calculations at one side of the worksheet may not be required in a final report.

HANDY TIP **Alternatively, click Print Area from the File menu and then click Set Print Area to specify a range of cells to print.**

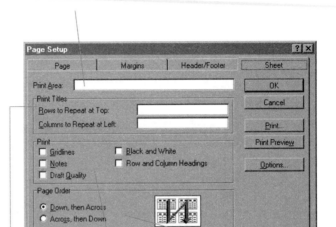

HANDY TIP **To resume printing the entire worksheet, click Print Area from the File menu and then click Clear Print Area.**

Print: Various options can be checked/unchecked.

Print Titles: A set of rows can be repeated at the top of each page or a set of columns can be repeated at the left of each page.

Page Order: Generally for wide spreadsheets it is more appropriate to print across first.

3 When complete, click OK.

Inserting Manual Page Breaks

Often, it is necessary to override the automatic page breaks inserted by Excel. The procedure for inserting page breaks manually is simple:

1. Select the row, column or cell at which the new page is to start, as follows:

To display automatic page breaks, click **Options** from the **Tools** menu and in the **View tab,** check the **Automatic Page Breaks box.**

Row: Select the row which is to form the top line of the next page.

Column: Select the column which is to form the left-most column of the next page.

Cell: Select the cell which is to form the top left cell of the next page.

In this example, row 45 is selected.

2. Click Page Break from the Insert menu.

	A	B	C	D	E	F	G	H	I	J
40										
41	Gross Profit									
42		Average Monthly Gross Profit =							£2,941.95	
43		Percentage of Sales =							42.7%	
44										
45	Expenses									
46		Accountancy	Annual Average =			£400.00				
47			Monthly Average =					£33.33		
48		Advertising	Annual Average =			£1,000.00				
49			Monthly Average =					£83.33		
50		Insurance	Annual Average =			£400.00				
51			Monthly Average =					£33.33		

You cannot remove automatic page breaks, only prevent their display.

3. To remove manual page breaks, make the selection as described at step 1 above and click Remove Page Break from the Insert menu.

Margins and Page Alignment

Click Page Setup from the File menu and click the Margins tab.

Margins: All margin, header and footer positions are measured from the paper edges.

Simply click the arrows to increment or decrement, or key in the distance required.

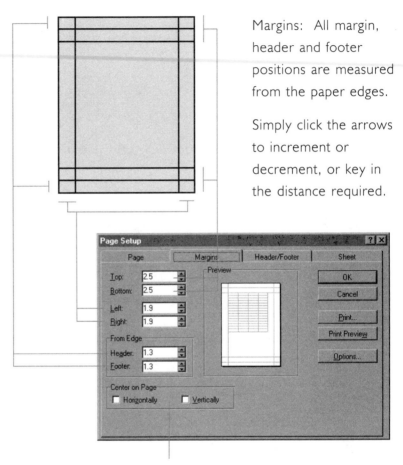

Page Alignment is usually to the left and to the top of the page. However, it can be centred either horizontally or vertically or both by checking the appropriate box(es).

Using Print Preview

To reduce trial and error and wasted paper, use Print Preview to view your work before printing it.

1 Click Print Preview from the File menu, or click the Print Preview button on the standard toolbar.

 By pointing to the margin lines and size handles, you can resize print area.

2 Click Zoom to get a close up view. Click again to return to normal view.

5 Click Margins to toggle the display of margins and size handles.

6 Click Close to return to worksheet display.

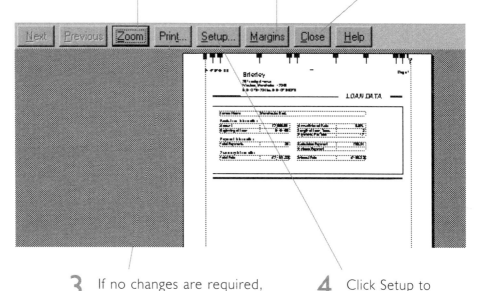

3 If no changes are required, click Print.

4 Click Setup to adjust page layout.

Headers and Footers

To create a header or a footer, carry out the following:

1 Click Page Setup from the File menu.

2 Click the Header/Footer tab.

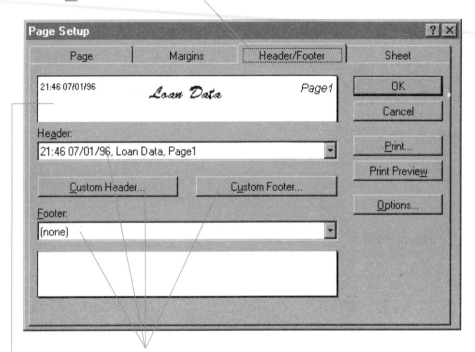

3 Select a header or footer from the list of built in headers and footers, or create your own header or footer by clicking the Custom Header or Custom Footer button.

4 A sample header or footer will be displayed in its format and location.

Custom Headers/Footers

The procedure for creating customized headers and footers is identical. The Dialogue box for a custom header is illustrated on the opposite page.

Page Number button inserts code for page number.

Date button inserts code for current date.

Filename button inserts code for name of workbook file.

Font button displays Font dialogue box.

Total Pages button inserts code for total number of pages in worksheet.

Time button inserts code for current time.

Sheet Name button inserts code for name of worksheet.

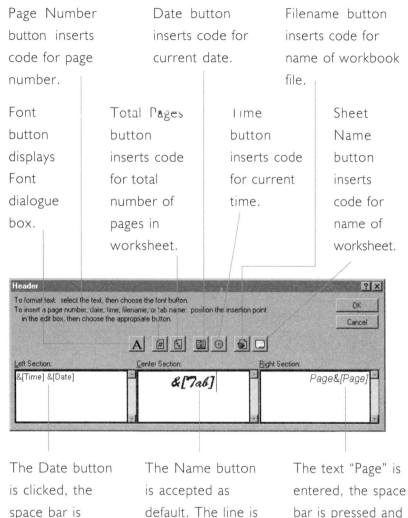

The Date button is clicked, the space bar is pressed and the Time button is clicked.

The Name button is accepted as default. The line is selected, the Font button clicked and the Font changed and made bold.

The text "Page" is entered, the space bar is pressed and the Page Number button is pressed.

File Print

1 Click Print from the File menu.

2 Choose what to print.

Click to set up options for the printer.

Click Selection to preselect cell ranges on selected sheets.

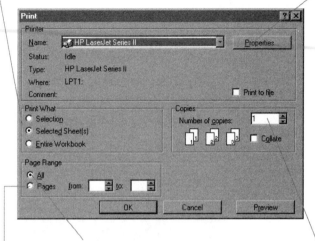

Click Selected Sheets to preselect a set of sheets, in which case print areas specified by the Page Setup Sheet tab or whole sheets will be printed.

3 Click to print the entire document.

or

4 Click and select or key in starting and finishing pages.

5 Click or key in the number of copies required.

6 Click OK.

CHAPTER THIRTEEN

Charts and Graphics

Excel enables you to create charts and graphs to summarise or to further analyse your worksheet data. It also provides a comprehensive range of graphic objects to enhance presentation. This is done very easily and quickly to achieve high graphic standards.

Covers

Creating a Chart

1 Select the data required in the chart.

	Qtr1	Qtr2	Qtr3	Qtr4	Totals
1991	£8,000	£10,000	£15,000	£12,000	£45,000
1992	£9,000	£11,000	£17,000	£13,000	£50,000
1993	£10,000	£12,000	£19,000	£14,000	£55,000
Totals	£27,000	£33,000	£51,000	£39,000	£150,000

HANDY TIP

To display the Chart toolbar, from the View menu select Toolbars and in the dialogue box check Chart.

2 Click the Chart Wizard button on the standard toolbar.

3 The worksheet pointer will change to fine cross-hairs with a small chart icon attached. Point it to one corner of the required chart and drag it to the opposite corner.

4 The first dialogue box of a sequence of five Chart Wizard dialogue boxes will be displayed.

HANDY TIP

To position the chart, click the location of the top left-hand corner and the chart will be sized automatically.

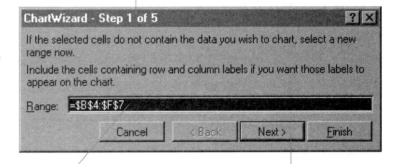

ChartWizard - Step 1 of 5

If the selected cells do not contain the data you wish to chart, select a new range now.

Include the cells containing row and column labels if you want those labels to appear on the chart.

Range: =$B$4:$F$7

Cancel < Back Next > Finish

5 If the selected range is incorrect, reselect the worksheet area.

6 Select Next to display the next dialogue box.

HANDY TIP

Select Finish to complete the chart with the default settings.

7 Select a type of chart. The default chart is highlighted.

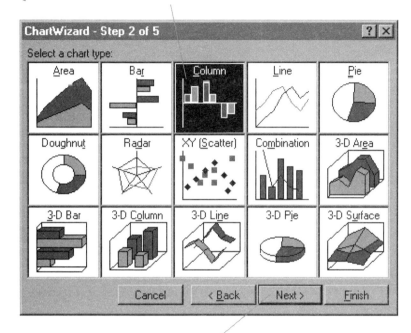

HANDY TIP **To return to the previous dialogue box, select Back.**

8 Select Next to display the next dialogue box.

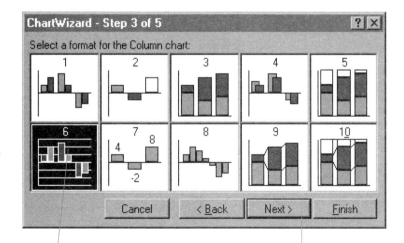

9 Select a format for the chart. The default format is highlighted.

10 Select Next to display the next dialogue box.

11 The order in which the selected data is plotted and which rows or columns will be used for the X-axis and legend is specified. Here the default is changed to columns so that years are used for the X-axis.

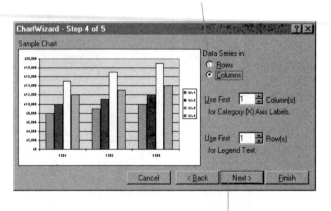

12 Click Next to display the next dialogue box.

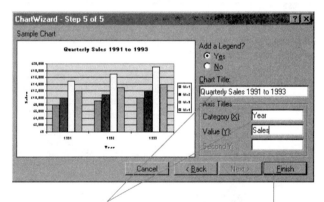

13 Enter the chart title and the axis titles.

14 Click Finish to produce the required chart.

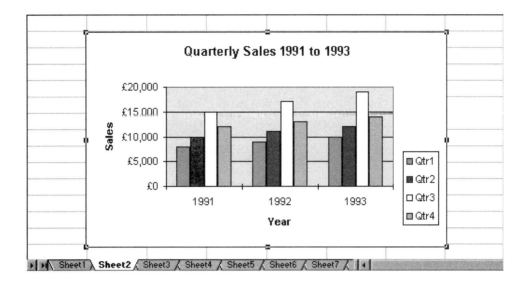

The chart produced is an embedded chart, since it is produced on the worksheet which contains the data. It is possible to produce a chart on a separate sheet in the workbook. The procedure is almost identical to creating an embedded chart, except that after the data range is selected, the following menu options are chosen:

HANDY TIP

The chart can be moved: point to anywhere inside the containing rectangle and drag to move it.

•   Insert menu

•   Chart sub-menu

•   As New Sheet option

Since the chart has sizing handles (small black boxes on the containing rectangle), it is said to be selected. As for any graphic object, it can be sized:

•   Drag the middle handles on the verticals to adjust width.

•   Drag the middle handles on the horizontals to adjust height.

•   Drag any corner to adjust overall size and hold down the Shift key to maintain the aspect ratio.

Activating/Selecting Charts

Chart Sheets are always activated, which means that the Chart menu bar is always displayed.

Embedded charts lie on a worksheet where the Command menu bar is normally displayed. To display the Chart menu bar, you must first activate the chart. Since the chart is a graphic object, it is also possible to select it.

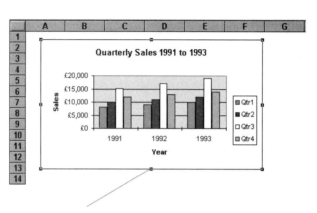

To de-activate or deselect the chart, click away from it anywhere on the worksheet.

To select an embedded chart, click it once anywhere within the chart so that the sizing handles appear on its border.

Note, the Chart Command menu bar is active.

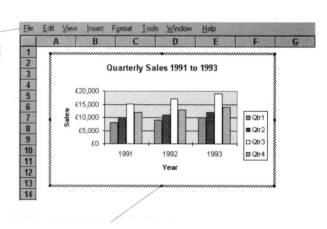

To activate an embedded chart, double-click so that its border changes to a thick grey line and sizing handles appear.

Chart Commands

Chart Toolbar

When a chart is selected or activated, the Chart toolbar is displayed.

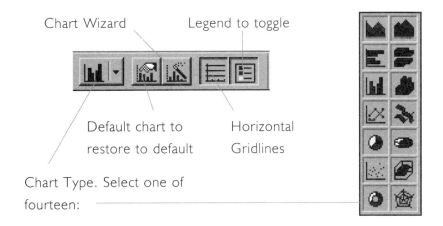

Chart Wizard

Legend to toggle

Default chart to restore to default

Horizontal Gridlines

Chart Type. Select one of fourteen:

Chart Command Menu

The Chart Command menu structure is very similar to the Worksheet Command menu structure, apart from the Insert and Format menus, which contain many new commands relating to charts.

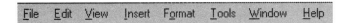

File Edit View Insert Format Tools Window Help

Inserting Extra Data

To insert extra data:

1 Introduce extra rows/columns and extra data, e.g. extra data points for 1994 quarterly sales.

	Qtr1	Qtr2	Qtr3	Qtr4	Totals
1991	£8,000	£10,000	£15,000	£12,000	£45,000
1992	£9,000	£11,000	£17,000	£13,000	£50,000
1993	£10,000	£12,000	£19,000	£14,000	£55,000
1994	£11,000	£13,000	£21,000	£15,000	£60,000
Totals	£27,000	£33,000	£51,000	£39,000	£150,000

2 Select the new range of cells.

3 Point to the boundary of the selected cells so that the pointer changes to an arrow and drag onto the chart area, where the pointer will have a small plus sign attached.

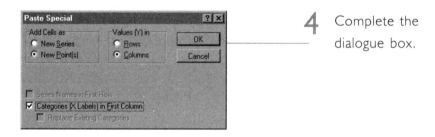

4 Complete the dialogue box.

5 On releasing the mouse button, the chart will be reconstructed with the data points for 1994.

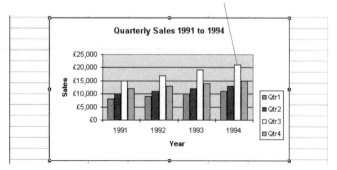

Formatting Charts

The procedure for formatting a chart is as follows:

1 Activate the chart.

2 Select the part of the chart to be formatted, either by clicking once with the mouse or by using the keyboard arrow keys.

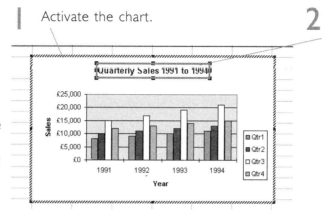

 An alternative method of formatting part of a chart is to double-click the part with the mouse.

3 Click Format from the Chart Command menu and then click Selected Chart Title or Selected Axis, etc.

4 An appropriate dialogue box will be displayed. Select the required tab and complete it.

 The currently selected item will be displayed on the formula bar.

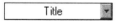

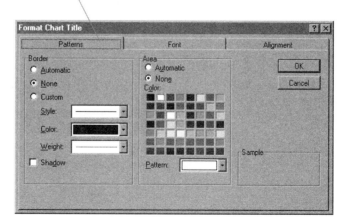

Adding Extra Text

The procedure for adding extra elements to a chart is as follows:

1 Click Insert from the Chart Command menu, and select the option for the element to be inserted, e.g. Titles, Data Labels, Legend, Axes, Gridlines, Picture, Trendline, Error Bars, New Data.

2 An appropriate dialogue box will be displayed.

Inserting Text

To edit text, click it once to select it and click it again to put it in editing mode.

The easiest element to insert in a chart is text, though this does not appear on the Insert menu. The procedure is as follows:

1 Select the chart.

2 Key in the text, e.g. "Note the peak in the third quarter".

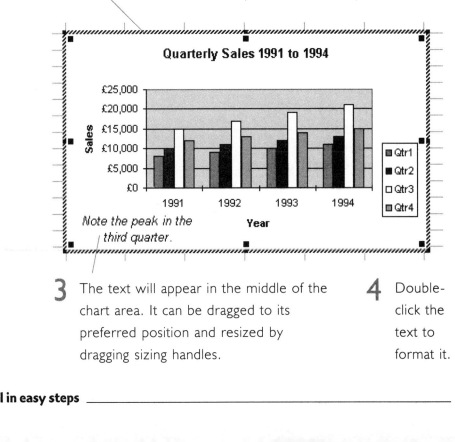

3 The text will appear in the middle of the chart area. It can be dragged to its preferred position and resized by dragging sizing handles.

4 Double-click the text to format it.

Custom AutoFormats

When you use Chart Wizard to choose a chart type and a sub-type, you are actually applying a Built-in AutoFormat which as well as giving you the chart type, also provides chart formatting. You can create Custom AutoFormats as follows:

1 Create a chart and format it.

2 Click Format from the Chart Command menu and then click the AutoFormat option.

3 The AutoFormat dialogue box will be displayed with the built in formats. Click User-Defined.

4 Click the Customize button and in the User-Defined AutoFormats dialogue box, click Add.

 Custom Auto-Formats can be deleted using the User Defined AutoFormats dialogue box. You are not allowed to delete Built-in AutoFormats.

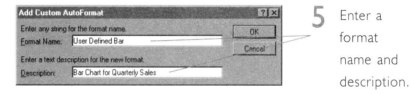

5 Enter a format name and description.

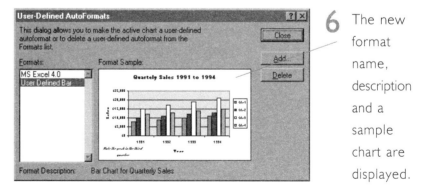

6 The new format name, description and a sample chart are displayed.

7 To apply the custom AutoFormat, activate the chart, select AutoFormat from the Format menu, select User-Defined and select the required custom format.

Using Graphic Objects

You may construct graphic objects on your worksheets and charts to further annotate and improve the presentation. A substantial range of objects and features are available on the Drawing toolbar which can be displayed from the standard toolbar.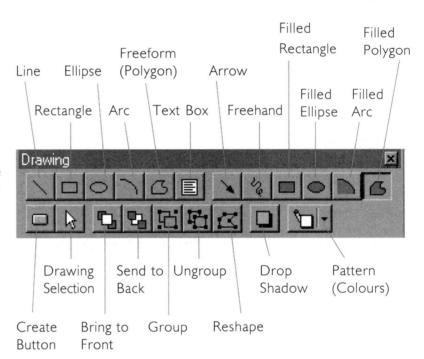

 To use a drawing tool once, click its button once. To use repeatedly, double-click its button; then, when you're finished, cancel by clicking the button again.

To draw an object, the procedure is as follows:

For rectangles, ellipses, arcs and text boxes	For lines and arrows
Drag the containing rectangle from one corner to the opposite corner.	Drag from one end to the other.

CHAPTER FOURTEEN

Macros and Customizing

A macro is a pre-specified sequence of commands, which Excel executes automatically. As soon as you start to routinely carry out repetitive sequences of commands, you will realise that you need a macro to store the sequence so that it can be replaced by a single command.

Excel allows you to customize toolbars so that you can change the buttons on the built-in toolbars and create new toolbars to display the buttons you use most often. It is also possible to create your own buttons.

Covers

Recording a Macro

In the following example, a macro will be recorded to make a selected cell bold, italic and underlined.

1 Select the cell: | Quarterly Sales |

2 Start the Macro Recorder by:

Clicking the Record Macro button on the Visual Basic toolbar.

or

Clicking Record Macro from the Tools menu and then Record New Macro.

To display the Visual Basic toolbar, select Toolbars from the View menu and check Visual Basic.

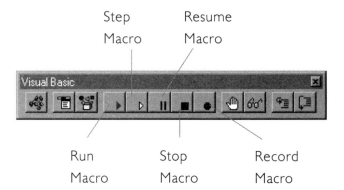

Step Macro   Resume Macro

Run Macro   Stop Macro   Record Macro

Normally a macro is recorded for many steps. Prior to recording, plan what you want to do and the exact sequence. Maybe try a pre-recording trial run?

3 Click the Options button on the Record New Macro dialogue box.

4 Enter the macro name. 5 Enter a description.

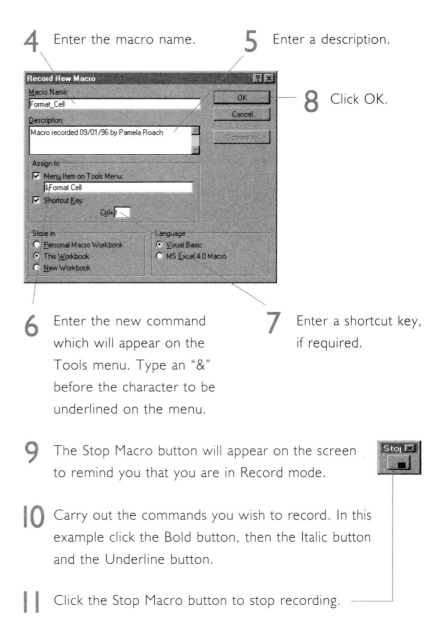

8 Click OK.

6 Enter the new command which will appear on the Tools menu. Type an "&" before the character to be underlined on the menu.

7 Enter a shortcut key, if required.

9 The Stop Macro button will appear on the screen to remind you that you are in Record mode.

10 Carry out the commands you wish to record. In this example click the Bold button, then the Italic button and the Underline button.

11 Click the Stop Macro button to stop recording.

Running a Macro

There are several ways of running a macro. For example, consider running the macro recorded in the previous section:

1 Select the cell to be processed.

2 Click Macro from the Tools menu.

or

Click the Run Macro button on the Visual Basic toolbar.

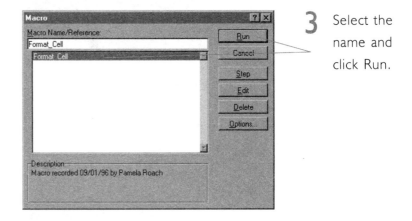

3 Select the name and click Run.

Alternatively,

4 Click the new command Format Cell from the Tools menu. Remember also the menu shortcut Alt+T followed by F.

or

Use the keyboard shortcut Ctrl+F.

Assigning Macros to Buttons

Excel's in-built customizing features allow you to create buttons to execute your macros, either on a particular worksheet or chart or more conventionally on a toolbar.

| Click the Create Button button on the Drawing toolbar.

2 Drag the mouse from corner to corner to construct the button.

3 Select the macro name and click OK.

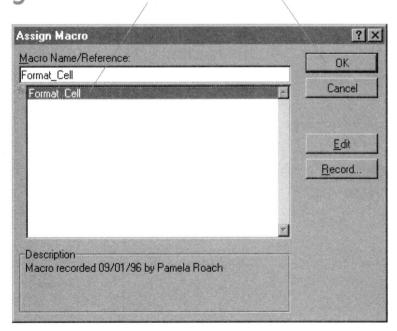

4 Edit and format the text on the button.

Creating Custom Toolbars

I Click Toolbars from the View menu.

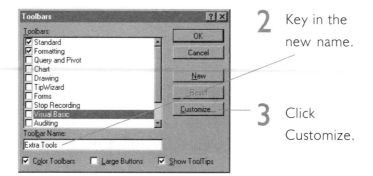

2 Key in the
new name.

3 Click
Customize.

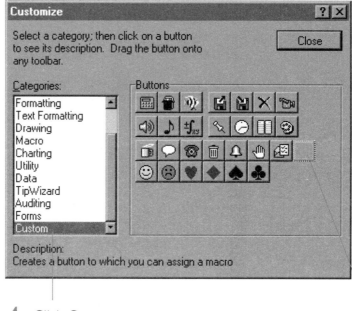

4 Click Custom.

5 Drag the empty button onto the new toolbar,
which will have appeared on the spreadsheet.

...contd

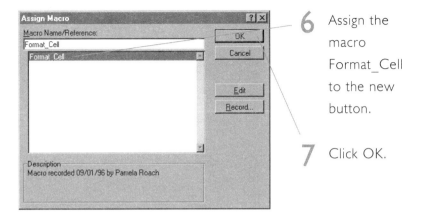

6   Assign the macro Format_Cell to the new button.

7   Click OK.

8   Select the Formatting category.

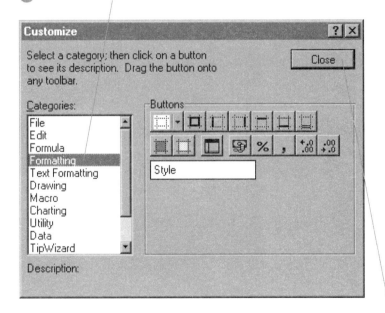

9   Drag the Percent Style button, Currency Style button and Borders button to the new toolbar.

10   Click Close.

Editing Button Image

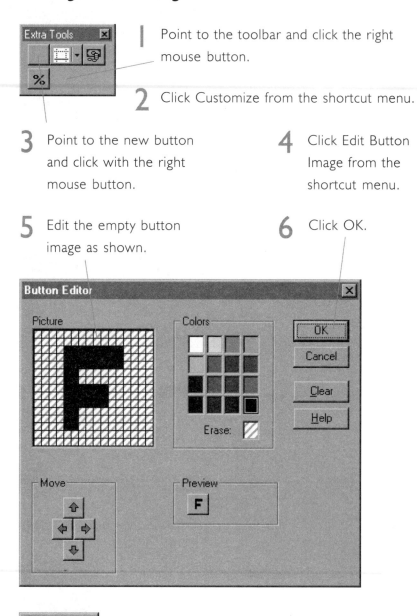

1 Point to the toolbar and click the right mouse button.

2 Click Customize from the shortcut menu.

3 Point to the new button and click with the right mouse button.

4 Click Edit Button Image from the shortcut menu.

5 Edit the empty button image as shown.

6 Click OK.

Index

R

S

T

U

W